IN PLAIN SIGHT

✦

The Story of TASK

- Trenton Area Soup Kitchen -

Lee Seglem

iUniverse, Inc.

New York Lincoln Shanghai

IN PLAIN SIGHT
The Story of TASK

Copyright © 2007 by Lee Seglem

iUniverse books may be ordered through booksellers or by contacting:

iUniverse
2021 Pine Lake Road, Suite 100
Lincoln, NE 68512
www.iuniverse.com
1-800-Authors (1-800-288-4677)

Because of the dynamic nature of the Internet, any Web addresses or links contained in this book may have changed since publication and may no longer be valid.

The views expressed in this work are solely those of the author and do not necessarily reflect the views of the publisher, and the publisher hereby disclaims any responsibility for them.

ISBN: 978-0-595-42758-1 (pbk)
ISBN: 978-0-595-69964-3 (cloth)
ISBN: 978-0-595-87088-2 (ebk)

Printed in the United States of America

For Joanne
And for Jeremy and Bret
We are so lucky

Contents

Preface

I live in a verdant slice of suburban America along the Delaware River about 30 miles northeast of Philadelphia, Pa. By any measure, my town, Lower Makefield, population 32,000, is a good place to raise a family. The median annual household income is in the neighborhood $100,000. The homes are comfortable, the streets well-lit, the crime rate low. In spring and summer, people plant flowers, mow lawns (or have them mowed) and watch their kids chase fireflies. Fall and winter bring soccer tournaments and crisp smoky air, bright lights and generous visits from Santa Claus. We have a public golf course, a community pool and a recreation system second to none. Property taxes are on the high end, but so is convenience. Within a three-mile radius of the township building, landscaped office parks bulge with every kind of doctor, dentist and therapist under the sun. There are houses of worship for every leading religious persuasion, banks for every checking preference and food stores for every culinary need. Not long ago, one big-box supermarket in town sought a permit to stay open 24 hours a day.

Such is life in the lap of historic Bucks County, where farm fields fade into sprawl and weathered stone manses stoop in the shadow of McMansions.

Drive north along the Delaware for five or ten miles, then cross the river into New Jersey heading east, then south and west in a broad arc forming the rough circumference of a circle, and you will pass through a succession of residential and commercial venues of similar self-secure circumstance: Washington Crossing, New Hope and Solebury on the Pennsylvania side, and in New Jersey, Lambertville, Hopewell, Pennington, Princeton, Lawrenceville, West Windsor and Hamilton—an impressive array of zip codes, to be sure. But amid the shared affluence and proximate location of these communities in relation to one another, there is a phenomenon no one much likes to talk about, even though it is as plain as the map on the wall: collectively, these locales form a ring of wealth and abundance around a place that has very little of either. That place is called Trenton, no less the capital city of New Jersey, one of wealthiest states in the nation, and, once upon a time, a booming manufacturing and urban retail center in its own right—but now very much the portal to another world just beyond our trim and tidy backyards.

From any point on this geographic compass of prosperity, you can drive into this other world and in a matter of minutes be among people who cannot afford a decent meal. Their lives are fractured by poverty, disability, illness, unemployment, hard luck, drug abuse, old age, neglect, bad judgment or some combination of all of that, and they stand in line every day counting on the kindness of strangers to put a plate of hot food in their hands. Some have jobs but walk a tightrope between paying rent and eating. Others are so far off the grid they spend the night in abandoned buildings or under bridges. Talk with them, and they speak of food in the context of survival.

The swiftness of the transition to this world is surreal, a trip so abrupt you might as well be flipping some weird kind of switch. Just as quickly as you arrived, you can drive away and be back on your deck sipping a drink or waiting for a latte in Starbucks or shopping at Wegmans or hiking in the woods or tucking into a deep-dish pizza at the Olive Garden, listening as a person at the table next to you looks at the menu and casually says, "I'm starving." To the uninitiated, crossing this divide can be unnerving, frightening even. To someone who has gone over and back time and again, watching the face of need loom in the windshield, then quickly recede in the rearview mirror—but never really go away—it is an experience that, over time, puts quite a lot of things in perspective.

Hunger, of course, is not unique to Trenton; communities around it have pockets of need as well, some of it substantial. And I certainly don't mean to imply that hunger is a defining social condition of this proud old commercial hub, which is struggling—with some measure of success—to reinvent itself and which faces enough challenges without needless negative exaggeration by some nattering out-of-towner. It would also be patently ridiculous to suggest that the city's municipal neighbors, or, for that matter, the thriving suburbs of any city, somehow contrive to foist hunger and want upon their urban counterpart. These problems and the tangled web of social, political, economic and moral issues that cause and sustain them are far too complicated for anything quite that simplistic. I will also stipulate that I am not nearly so naïve or uninformed as to think that hunger is somehow confined to a single state, region or nation, or that it is no worse elsewhere. Of course it is. Even school children know about killer famines that periodically ravage great swaths of humanity across the planet.

But all of that said, Trenton is where I learned about hunger, where it became personal for me, where it shed a thick hide of abstraction and touched my life, if only from the outside looking in. It is also where I learned something else: that the kindness of strangers can make a difference, even against a scourge that lingers in plain sight and never goes away.

That is why I wrote this book.

•   •   •

My introduction to what bureaucrats and policy wonks dispassionately, and with a certain Orwellian flair, refer to these days as "food insecurity" or "food insufficiency"—and to what is being done about it in this small corner of the world—came early one afternoon in 1999 when I went for a walk across town. I work for Trenton's largest employer, the State of New Jersey, and for several years had been donating money through the annual State Employees Charitable Campaign to something called the Trenton Area Soup Kitchen. "TASK," as it was dubbed in the campaign literature, sounded like a worthwhile cause, but I had never been there, and the image in my mind's eye was stuck on a bleak Depression-era stereotype of bread lines and grim-faced men shuffling around in tattered overcoats. I decided to have a look.

No sooner had I gotten within a hundred yards of the building that houses TASK when a glimpse into the fundamental nature and reputation of the place preceded my arrival. A woman who happened to be headed in the same direction approached me on the street and, before I had a chance to even think about exercising the usual avoidance-of-panhandling reflex, she was in my face—but not for money. Rather, she seemed genuinely curious about where I was going. When I told her, she launched into a monologue about some of the practicalities of being poor in the city, and as we walked along together, it quickly became apparent that TASK was definitely on the plus side of her meager ledger. When we reached the wide open front door, her parting words were about the food: "They feed you real good here. Real good." And with that, she smiled and stepped inside.

I followed a few moments later and was immediately struck by brightness. Sunlight streaming through a bank of windows to my right illuminated a large rectangle of space filled with tables and chairs. Colorful artwork hung the entire length of the wall running beneath the windows, and as I scanned the room, I noticed that every available nook on every wall seemed to boast paintings and drawings of one sort or another. Directly ahead, on the far side of an expanse of tables, stood a glass and metal structure resembling the food service counter of a school cafeteria, only smaller. Behind it, framed by a pass-through in the wall, I could see people wiping down ovens and metal table tops and mopping the floor. Lunch was winding down, and a few people lingered, talking quietly in clusters. Off to one side, a man sorted through a table covered with magazines and paperback books, free for the taking. Across the way, someone surveyed a bulletin board tacked full of announcements, service ads and phone numbers.

I thought, *This is a soup kitchen? It looks and feels like a community center.*

Abruptly, I was approached by a tall man wearing khakis, a polo shirt and the cordial but scrutinizing expression of someone whose job obviously included finding out what was the deal with this bewildered stranger loitering in his midst. I will not soon forget this first meeting with Peter Wise, TASK's executive director at the time. That is, in part, because I completely misread the man, just as I had the woman who'd approached me on the way in, just as I had the whole notion of what a soup kitchen was supposed to look like. Maybe it was the fact that he appeared so comfortable and at ease in these surroundings, or maybe it was the authoritative, staccato description he gave of the mechanics of feeding several hundred desperate people every day. In any event, I immediately pegged Wise for a guy in the thick of a long career in urban social work. In fact, as I would learn much later on, he had been at TASK's helm for less than 18 months and, like me, was a product of that outlying suburban/professional milieu. He'd spent most of his adult life as an engineer and aerospace industry manager, helping to design satellites of all things. When the company down-sized and pulled out of town, Wise took note of his age and circumstance and decided to retire—then wound up running a soup kitchen because, spiritually, he believed he was "called" to do just that.

So much for first impressions. But as I would also learn in time, that's the way it is at TASK. First impressions, conventional wisdom, preconceived notions—the usual games of expectation and pre-judgment that tend in so many situations to be long on assumption and short on facts—are particularly vulnerable to inaccuracy inside the four walls of a place like this. And as for the bit about being "called" to serve, I don't consider myself a religious person, and Wise, when he mentioned it, wasn't wearing religion on his sleeve; in fact, I haven't met many people around TASK who do. But I will say this: it does make you wonder. As I came to be more deeply acquainted with TASK and with those who define its existence on a daily basis I was struck repeatedly by how threads of chance and circumstance in life are sometimes arranged—by fate, serendipity, dumb luck, a "higher power," call it what you will—to put people in positions that make a difference for others.

As the last of the lunchtime diners trickled out and the chairs were being stacked, the tables cleaned for the day, I asked about volunteer opportunities, and Wise ticked off a range of options—prepping in the kitchen, filling trays on the serving line, tutoring, mentoring, raising money, donating food, the list went on. No hard sell, just an open invitation to help. After ten minutes or so, we shook hands, and as I walked out the door heading back across town to my office, one thing he told me played over in my mind.

"We serve people unconditionally," he said. "No questions asked. No one is ever turned away."

A week or so later, I went back; in fact, I made it a bit of a habit. As the months went by, one volunteer stint led to another, and eventually I was asked to serve on the organization's governing board. Then one day, when my back was turned (just kidding), my fellow trustees elected me chairman.

•   •   •

Much has happened since I first crossed the threshold of 72½ Escher Street that summer day in 1999. Indeed, much has changed since I started filling the very pages of this book in 2006, highlighted by Peter Wise's retirement after a record eight years at the helm and, in his place, the arrival of a garrulous, committed social-service veteran in the person of Dennis Micai, whose attitude and approach can be summed up by what he told a local newspaper, only half-jokingly, upon stepping up. "At some point," Micai said, "I'd like to put us out of business."

He's got his work cut out. New programs continue to be launched and others expanded, the staff is larger, and TASK is a busier place all around. Beyond serving as Trenton's only weekday soup kitchen, the organization spends a good deal of time and money fostering self-sufficiency through adult education, computer training, life-skills instruction, award-winning arts programs and multi-dimensional social-service counseling. Keeping pace with this requires hard work and aggressive fund-raising, and TASK relies heavily upon on a small legion of dedicated volunteers and generous donors who help sustain an annual operating budget approaching $2 million—a budget that has quadrupled over the past decade. Incidentally, more than 80 cents of every dollar underwrites activities and services directly beneficial to those in need. And one key measure of just how broadly this service spectrum has evolved is that the organization was forced by burgeoning circumstance in recent years to undertake a major expansion of its physical plant to provide more space to serve more people.

All in all, not bad for a small nonprofit whose troubled and humble beginnings once had it serving soup and sandwiches from the confines of a dusty vacant lot.

But not altogether good, either.

Before we get too warm and fuzzy about all of this, let's not lose sight of what is really going on here, what is driving the need for such laudatory and uplifting community service.

TASK was founded in 1982 to feed the hungry, and that remains the primary mission. Over the years, it has served more than two million hot and cold meals and, beyond that, has distributed veritable tons of unprepped dry goods, fruit, bread and other foodstuffs, one can, jar, box and bag at a time. Despite occasional minor dips from month to month, the overall demand has risen steadily year after year. Indeed, with 2007 marking the 25th anniversary of the very first lunch served by TASK, the organization was within shouting distance of yet another stunning milestone—200,000 meals in a single year. And it's not just TASK. Food banks, pantries and other providers of supplemental and emergency nutrition of every shape and size are all grappling with the same disturbing trend.

So it doesn't take a genius to recognize the underside of what is happening here: the soup kitchen is growing, in large part, because the problem that gave rise to it in the first place—"food insecurity," "food insufficiency," hunger by any other name—is growing. In fact, were hunger a legitimate economic enterprise, it might well be appropriately listed on Wall Street as a growth industry, a 21st Century growth industry no less, thriving in broad daylight in one of the richest states in the wealthiest nation on the face of the earth.

Why do we tolerate this? What if someone, some diabolically clever entrepreneur say, were to pick up on this sort of growth and run with it? Actually attempt to position hunger as a profit-making venture, recruit investors, try to sell stock in it? What would happen then? I'd be willing to bet a paycheck—hell, a couple of paychecks—that even some of the hardest of hearts among us would be aghast at such a scheme. That politicians of every stripe, egged on by the media, would denounce it as an outrage. That it would be driven out of business faster than you can say "morally reprehensible."

But why wait for some greed-crazed entrepreneur to provide the pretext? Dennis Micai's got it right: why not put this miserable business of hunger out of business just the way it is, right there in front of us, right now?

Will we ever find the courage and the commitment to do that?

As I write this, the television flickers with images of talking heads yammering back and forth about the outcome and implications of the most recent national election cycle. Control of the Congress has shifted, Washington is a different place, and change is in the wind as we head into another presidential year. So they say. Indeed, some pundits have gone so far as to suggest that we're on the leading edge of a period of progressive activism to rival the economic and political change that swept the United States a full century ago. Back when shameful revelations of widespread poverty and privation in the midst of plenty—"how that other half lives" in the words of famed muckraker Jacob Riis—grabbed America by the lapels and inspired it to do the right thing, compassionately and in pursuit of genuine social reform. On the other hand, with the current public agenda still largely drowned out by the booming twin voices of war and terror, it is not at all clear when, or even whether, we will insist on revisiting poverty or hunger or the nation's widening economic and social disparities for a new and long-overdue discussion of practical solutions. So, another Progressive Era? We'll see.

In the meantime, what I've tried to do here is put a human face on one small corner of this neglected agenda in the hope, perhaps, of promoting that discussion. As I said, I am not a scientist, social or otherwise, and I don't purport to present myself as any sort of technical expert in these matters. One thing this book is not is a compilation of heavy-duty academic or socio-economic analysis. That I'll leave to genuine, fully-qualified policy wonks. I'm a reporter, a writer and a volunteer. I feel strongly about this issue and make no pretense about that. I undertook this project because I thought it important to offer an unvarnished, uncomplicated account of a phenomenon that many of us don't think about but should. So pardon my advocacy. More than anything, though, this is really just a simple story about everyday people. People who need help and people who are fighting a holding action to meet that need.

Fortunately, and unfortunately, that fight goes on.

Lower Makefield, Pa.
August 2007

1

A Day in the Life

Quarter to seven on a chilly spring morning, and the Trenton Area Soup Kitchen, like much of the city that surrounds it, is waking up and trying to stay warm. Lucky for everyone who relies on this place, Sam Johnson and his crew are ahead of the game on both counts. The ovens are cranked up to 350 degrees, and a portable radio perched on the spice shelf is cranked even higher. Stainless steel tables at the center of the food prep area are heaped with the raw material for a lunch that will be built around spaghetti with meat sauce, and the staff already have their hands full: Loretta, on soup duty, is emptying cans of cream of mushroom soup into a large aluminum kettle; Bruce, taking charge of the beverage department, is mixing several vats of fruit punch; Jennifer, shuttling from refrigerator to oven to stove top, is pulling together a breakfast of scrambled eggs and waffles.

They've been at it since dawn, when Sam turned a key in the front door, stepped inside and quickly tapped at a coded keypad to deactivate the building's alarm system. Crossing the dimly lit dining area, past rows of tables stacked with folded metal chairs, past the cafeteria-style serving area, he entered the kitchen proper, flicked on the lights, turned on a large-urn coffee maker and set about the first critical order of business—checking temperatures inside the walk-in refrigerator and an adjacent freezer. These vault-like machines contain a fair portion of TASK's answer to hunger on any given day: ground beef, chicken, fresh and frozen vegetables and fruit, sauces, trays of pre-made side dishes, salads and, depending upon the season—especially around the Thanksgiving and Christmas holidays—maybe a quarter-ton's worth of whole frozen turkeys stacked precariously in the freezer like slippery bowling balls. Unmonitored, the agglomeration of wires, coils and other gizmos that power the cooling systems could easily fail, and the failure could go undetected for hours, quite possibly spoiling several hundred pounds of chicken and rice, beans, mac and cheese—whatever happens to be on the menu any given day. The staff takes this part of the job seriously; every morning, following a strict schedule, they log the temperatures on charts fixed to clipboards that hang from each unit. "This is critical because of possible food poisoning," Sam says. "We have to be very careful."

Satisfied the gauges show no sign of having strayed into the red overnight, the crew turns their full attention to the main event: cooking for a crowd, the leading edge of which will walk through the front door in a few hours. Today, they will cut, chop, boil, fry, pour, scramble and clean up for a turnout that could go as high as 400 for lunch, plus breakfast for students enrolled in TASK's adult education program. Later, a second shift will prep for supper on the expectation that as many as 200 will queue up on the serving line. The kitchen will also prepare, package and deliver at least 120 evening meals to a location across town where TASK has established a satellite facility in the city's south end. Estimating meal counts in advance, however, can be tricky business. As a general rule, demand is lower at the beginning of the month when welfare and other forms of assistance put hard cash into empty pockets and fewer people need supplemental food. Two or three weeks in, sometimes sooner, the numbers grow steadily larger, and as the waning days of the month approach, the soup kitchen often becomes a jammed, frenetic train station at rush hour, serving three or four times as many meals as at the start—upwards of 800 in a single day.

This being a Wednesday in the run-up to Easter, the count could go either way, but Sam, TASK's kitchen supervisor, is confident of the projections, and he takes command of the main course. Flanked by crates of tomato sauce, deep trays of chopped onions and green peppers and a pair of trunk-sized plastic bins—one laden with 10-pound bags of ground beef, the other sprouting a spindly heap of raw pasta—he turns the dial on a control box and fires up an open cooker. A cousin to the ovens, this ungainly device, essentially a large, waist-high metal tub on a hinge that tilts for draining, is about as close to an essential piece of equipment as you'll find here, employed daily to braise, boil and steam huge batches of rice, potatoes, vegetables and more. Sam sets about filling it now with chopped meat, followed by three large jars of minced garlic, salt and pepper and a fistful of spices. When the meat starts to brown, he reaches for an aluminum paddle and vigorously stirs the sizzling mixture, a cloud of pungent, steamy smoke swirling upward under the pull of an exhaust fan. Like any chef worth his salt, he likes to talk about cooking while he cooks, and he launches into a brief riff about flavor, presentation and color, especially color: "I try to make it so the colors contrast with each other when we put the food out. It needs to look good on the serving line." Today, green beans will lean up against the spaghetti, along with tossed salad and some fruit, probably from a huge cache of fresh red grapes donated yesterday, chilling now in the cooler.

"I know this is a soup kitchen," Sam observes, stating the obvious—in a tone that adds an unmistakable *but so what.* "I want to use my skills to make the food here look and taste good." Besides, he says, motioning toward the dining area, "I don't put anything out there that I wouldn't personally eat myself."

Tall and talkative with a West African lilt and a face at home with laughter, Sam landed at TASK from an unusual trajectory. Born Samuel Timiekpedegha in a small town in southern Nigeria (he later adopted his father's Anglicized surname, Johnson, in place of that tongue-twister, which he says made him the brunt of school-yard teasing), he left home after high school to work at a bank in Lagos, the capital. It was a good job in a big city, but Sam found it impossible to ignore a nagging childhood dream—learning to fly. And so he bounded out of the teller's cage and chased that dream all the way to Europe, enrolling in a Belgian flight school, studying French on the side. In time, though, the dream proved bigger than the wallet, and he ran out of money. Flight certificate out of reach, he drifted, staying afloat on meager income from odd jobs. One day, he walked into a high-brow Brussels restaurant—and met his future. At first, it was as humble and uninspiring as it gets: washing dishes, scrubbing pots, serving as kitchen go-fer. But after a while, after experiencing the daily rhythms of the place, the magic of common foods transformed into edible works of art and, most memorably, the friendliness of a chef "who took me under his wing and trained me," something inside clicked. "Back home, you know, I used to help my mom with cooking, but I didn't know it could be a career until I went to Europe."

Then he set his sights on America, traveling the country, working in restaurants large and small, eventually settling in New Jersey where he refined his cookery in commercial kitchens along the Route 1 corridor from Princeton to New Brunswick. He saved money and made connections and in 1997 launched a small catering business from his Willingboro home, cutting a deal with a popular Trenton club, Katmandu, that gave him use of its kitchen during off hours. He was there early on a sunny September morning in 2001 when he heard anguished voices and rushed out to find shocked colleagues glued to a television, watching an airliner crash into the World Trade Center.

Over the next few weeks, the horrifying images swirling in his head, Sam felt compelled to do something tangible. "I watched what was happening, and I started to think of the need and the people working at ground zero. How were they being fed? I couldn't get an answer, so I got in my car. Most of my friends said I was crazy, but I said, 'I bet I'll get into the city.'" Police stopped him at the Holland Tunnel, but he persisted, pleading, cajoling, at one point even displaying photographs showing him with a former New Jersey governor for whom he had once catered an official event. Finally, the cops relented. They let him through under escort to a place in Lower Manhattan called Nino's, a Canal Street restaurant transformed into an emergency canteen for rescue workers toiling in the wreckage blocks away. Starting out as an auxiliary cook in what by then had become a round-the-clock, 7,000-meal-a-day frenzy, Sam eventually was put on the payroll in charge of the kitchen, where he presided over an eclectic cavalcade of volunteers, including a blur of cameos by celebrities, politicians and government dignitaries, many of whom he didn't recognize. The memory of one such encounter makes him laugh. "One day, there was this guy helping in the kitchen, and I was ordering him around, telling him to take out the trash, do this, do that, and he was doing everything I told him to, and I had no idea who he was." It turned out to be Louis Freeh, the former FBI director. Over time, Sam became something of a mini-celebrity in his own right, recognized and popular among the rescue crews, featured in news stories. Ask, and he'll pull out a sheaf of clips to prove it.

Returning to Jersey some five months later, he turned down the offer of a higher-paying job at a top-drawer restaurant in favor of an opportunity at the soup kitchen, and it is no mystery to him why he made that choice. "It lets me use my skills to feed this kind of population that is in need. It's like giving back to the community." Besides, he says, TASK is closer to home, the hours are better, and, compared to the volume of food he was dishing out during those long and stressful days and nights in New York City at the edge of a nation's pierced heart, "this is just like a walk in the park for me."

•   •   •

It's a few minutes past eight, and sunshine streaming through windows high on the east wall of the dining area brings to life a colorful gallery of artwork that all but surrounds this space: paintings and photographs, portraits, landscapes, street scenes and abstracts, all produced by the very people who come here for help. In the center of the room, a stocky man wearing a navy wool cap emblazoned "USA" on the front is moving from table to table, systematically taking down and unfolding tan-and-gray metal chairs, deploying them three to a side, one at each end. He is Maximo Mendez, known to all as Mike, custodian, handyman and all around CEO of odd jobs, a veteran TASK employee who can recall when the soup kitchen wasn't really a kitchen at all but a rudimentary soup-and-sandwich enterprise run from the basement of a Trenton church.

As usual, Mike arrived on foot this morning after a 45-minute mini-trek from his home in the city's south end, a daily ritual he says he finds energizing even in bad weather and feeling the aches of advancing age. Today, the open-air commute was a piece of cake, calm, clear and brisk. "That's why I feel good," he says, his gray moustache curling with a smile.

Chairs in place, he starts wiping down the table tops, working quickly, almost as quickly as he speaks. "I do a little bit of everything, clean inside, outside, check the offices, make sure enough soap is in the bathrooms, sweep the floors, go into the kitchen, set out the trays, the cups, the paper towels, you name it. They don't have to tell me 'do this, do that,' nothing. It's already done."

Other staffers begin to trickle through the front door and, already, preparations are being made for the arrival of today's cadre of antici-pated volunteers. Every day, the organization must make sure it hooks up with enough outside help to prep food, serve meals, sort donated clothing, stock shelves, stuff fund-raising envelopes and complete a raft of other time-consuming, labor-intensive tasks beyond the limited reach and wherewithal of paid staff. Given TASK's deep and abiding base of regular volunteers—some 780 individuals from all around the greater Trenton area—one would think the challenge is simple: make a few calls and wait for people to show up. But it doesn't always work that way. Maintaining consistent numbers is difficult, staffers say. Some-times, groups either don't bring enough people or they bring too many. Not enough, and that could put a crimp in the food service and other functions. Too many, and there might not be enough for everyone to do, raising the problematic prospect that volunteers might go away wonder-ing why they came. Penciled in today are a contingent of students from the Lawrenceville School near Princeton and a handful of regulars from a Presbyterian church just across the Delaware River in Yardley, Pa.—overall, a small group with little margin for error. Still, if the num-bers come up short, there is always Plan B: if push comes to shove, the organization can always put staff on the serving line, a rare but not unprecedented exigency.

Abruptly, a buzzer sounds from the kitchen and someone shouts "Back door!"—signaling the arrival of a delivery. Bruce drops what he's doing and rushes down a short, narrow corridor toward the rear of the building. Rounding a corner, he throws his weight against the push-bar on a set of double doors, which fly open to reveal a garrulous, heavy-set man—Tom Reilly, a TASK volunteer known to some around here as "Santa Claus" (and not entirely without cause, given his dead-on holiday impersonation—genuine white beard and all.) This morning, though, he's all business. The soup kitchen's regular driver is laid up with complications from diabetes, and Tom has taken the wheel of TASK's van to maintain a circuit of daily visits to local stores that routinely donate day-old baked goods, produce and other unsold leftovers. Pointing toward the vehicle's compartment, which is crammed with bulging plastic bags, he offers good news and bad. It's a decent haul—copious amounts of donuts and pastries, some cakes and a bunch of boxed pies. But the van is a problem. "We hit two supermarkets, two bakeries—and one gas station." Tom says. "We got an oil leak, and I'm putting in two quarts a day."

Hoisting the cargo inside, Tom and Bruce stack it on metal racks just to the right of another set of doors that form the entrance to a small warehouse. The larger of two pantries maintained by TASK, this is the adopted domain of Jan Curran, a retired teacher and longtime volunteer who spends most mornings stacking, arranging and taking stock of a sprawling, ever-changing assemblage of canned and boxed food donations—a sort of dry-goods analogue to the walk-in coolers. "It's impossible to organize back here unless you're picking at it every day," she says, her attention at the moment focused on a peculiarity in one of the shelves. Normally filled with cans of soup, this space now is all but empty—an inauspicious irony and an example of spot shortages that periodically diminish various elements of the entire inventory. "This is a very slow time of year for us," perhaps even a bit slower than usual, Jan says. The Christmas rush, a flood of community generosity that typically overwhelms TASK's storage capacity, has ebbed with the advent of spring, and several natural disasters have dominated headlines—and the flow of charitable giving—in recent months. "I think a lot of people are just donated out; they've put forth a lot in a lot of places. Our regular donors, for example, people who just come in with cans of food or whatever, they're just dribbling in now."

Still, the place has the appearance of a large, utterly over-stuffed garage. Shelves stretch nearly floor to ceiling, supporting crates of juice and tomato sauce, tuna, cans of U.S. Department of Agriculture (USDA) surplus pork and potatoes, stew, beans, corn, rice—staples for the daily double of meals prepared in the kitchen. Facing these shelves is a wall of boxed crackers, cereal, cookies, bags of candy and other goodies routinely broken down and sorted into individual portions by volunteers for direct distribution to patrons. A nearby table brims with children's "breakfast bags," each containing a cold cereal, a packet of instant oatmeal, powered milk and a raisin or granola bar. One corner of shelf space is occupied by crates containing an unusual jumble of items for which the kitchen has little or no practical use, things like jars of artichoke hearts, canned beets, containers of apple sauce, boxes of cake and muffin mix, occasionally even the odd tin of pate or pot of marmalade. A few weeks ago, this potpourri of oddities had its own sentinel of sorts, a beribboned, cellophane-wrapped chocolate elf about the size of a fire plug. Misfits from well-intentioned donors, these culinary orphans nevertheless serve a purpose. "Every month or so," Jan says, "we bunch this kind of stuff together for special giveaways." (For the record, the "elf," which turned out to be hollow, was carefully fractured into hundreds of pieces and handed out as a supplemental dessert.)

Because TASK relies so heavily on donated food, much of it unsolicited, staff and volunteers have learned from experience that certain obvious precautions are in order. "The expiration dates are important, rotation is important—first in, first out, that sort of thing," Jan says. Sometimes, the avoidance of a potential problem comes down to simple chance fortified by careful observation. She recalls one instance in which a donor, having cleaned out the kitchen cabinets at home, dropped off several boxes of goods, including cranberry sauce in cans bearing labels that struck one volunteer as vaguely familiar—from memories of her youth. The product turned out to have been manufactured circa 1956. Often, expiration dates are encrypted in strings of digits useless to anyone unschooled in the technical argot of the food industry. "Here, look at this," Jan says, handing over a five-pound jar of generic peanut butter bearing nothing other than the number 230049. To untangle the meaning of sequences like this, staff has relied on the expertise of a volunteer who walked in one day and happened to mention she had become familiar with such codes during a stint in military procurement.

Most of what crosses this pantry's busy threshold, though, is good to go—and greatly appreciated. "All sorts of things," says Jan, "from boxes and cans of stuff you or I would bring in, to large corporate donations—that's really our anchor here. Sometimes, a company will bring a thousand bagged lunches all at once. You never know. That's what's interesting about this place: you never know what's coming in on any given day."

· · ·

The clock out front is just shy of nine, but already an unruly procession of mini-crises, loose ends and unresolved issues is pushing and stomping for attention around the cluttered desk of Cathy Ann Vandegrift, TASK's assistant director. Tom Reilly's given her an update on the van's oil problem, the upshot of which is probably another round of costly repairs on top of a recent (and partially botched) transmission job, not to mention the logistical headache of the vehicle being stuck back in the shop for a few days. Then there's the continuing telephone tag over an employee's disputed health-insurance coverage. And the paperwork to untangle bureaucratic confusion over welfare-related job search and work requirements. And here comes Sam with word that a small piece of equipment from the kitchen has gone missing. And someone just called offering three pallets of fruit juice, gratis—do we have space for it? And, by the way, don't forget to iron out final arrangements for Friday's Easter festivities—*who* was supposed to bring those 400 cupcakes?

"I come in here every day with my agenda," Cathy says, "but the soup kitchen usually has its own. And lately, I've just been putting out fires."

The office in which this controlled chaos is unfolding is not much bigger than the walk-in cooler just a few paces away—but don't be fooled by the size. Situated smack between the kitchen and dining area, with doors leading to both, this is TASK's nerve center, an area of little more than 100 square feet crammed with desks, filing cabinets, two computers, a fax machine, phones that ring a lot, shelves laden with equipment manuals, binders of budget and inventory data, meal-count records, boxes of Ramen Noodles waiting to be handed out, and, in a corner nook occupied by helpers who share this space with Cathy, the guts of the organization's volunteer operation. Scribbled phone numbers and reminders cover sticky notes that seem to be pasted everywhere. Bulletin boards are tacked full of work schedules, calendars and sundry instructions. This is where the food is ordered, the daily menus planned, the supplies tracked. Given its location, it is also the main intersection at TASK between immediate need and offers of relief or referral, and the traffic is very heavy. People who are homeless or who, for whatever reason, have no permanent address, have mail sent here. On busy days, the doorway frames face after desperate face voicing questions both impossibly large and manageably small: I just got out of prison, what should I do? How can I get an apartment? Got anything for a toothache? Can I have a bus pass? Any socks today? Band-aids? Q-tips? Tylenol?

Unflappable and even-tempered through it all, outwardly at least, the woman many patrons call "Miss Cathy" joined the staff in the late 90s, serving first as interim director during a period of leadership transition before settling into what amounts to one of the soup kitchen's most critical hands-on, multi-tasking roles. Her immediate background was in commercial real estate, but before that she spent about 16 years in the nonprofit world, serving as a psychological counseling aide. She credits the real estate experience with giving her an appreciation for work shaped by variety ("You never knew what the day was going to bring—a lot like this.") But it was the time spent dealing with young people overcome with mental distress that she says gave her the skills to navigate the tide of human affliction that gushes through TASK every day. "That's where I learned about boundaries," she says, "the ability to maintain a boundary with someone you're trying to help, to not feed into their problem or make it worse but at the same time to be very empathetic. As much a part of that is learning to assert authority without being over-bearing."

At the soup kitchen, what this means, among many other things, is having the savvy and the mettle to step into volatile situations that erupt from time to time and prevent them from spiraling out of control. Many who come here are already stressed to the breaking point by a stew of dysfunction, and it doesn't take much—an errant side-glance, say, or someone butting in line, or the mere perception of an errant side-glance or someone butting in line—to trigger a confrontation. Those who have watched Cathy get between angry patrons who are about to jump ugly with each other describe a portrait of courage and calmness, firmly applied.

"Boundaries" also means finding a way to maintain some distance between the fabric of your own sanity and the tattered spool of heart-rending circumstances that unravels before your eyes every day. And sometimes, she has found, this sort of boundary is quite impossible to maintain.

"One time, there was this sweet little boy, in second or third grade, whose mother drank and screamed at him all the time. In the summer, he would come here in the morning by himself and during the adult education class, he would work on his math. A social worker and I talked among ourselves about getting him out of that situation." Cathy talked it over with her husband, too, and one of the options they discussed was trying to enroll the child in a local parochial school at their own expense. "But the more we talked about it, the more we realized that unless we actually got him out of there, got him out of that home, nothing was really going to change. Anyway, since then, he's grown up and gotten involved in an armed robbery, and he's typical of what happens. Yet, you just knew he was going to get eaten alive out there and that he didn't really have a chance. That was very painful. That was the most difficult thing for me."

But there are those other moments. "There was a guy one time who used to come in either drunk or stoned and always antagonistic and belligerent. Well, he somehow cleaned up his act and moved to Brooklyn and got a commercial driving license to drive long-haul rigs around the country. Once or twice a year, he stops by to say hello. That's really nice." And then there are those who just say thank you. "One afternoon a few years ago, this guy was sitting outside on a milk crate, and someone came running in to say he was having a problem, having chest pains. I called 911. That was it, that's all I did. But as far as he was concerned, I saved his life. And every chance he gets, he still tells people I saved his life."

•   •   •

The wall of Cathy's cubicle facing the dining area is dominated by a large picture window, which, at the moment, circumscribes a scene of open books on tables occupied by two dozen or so pencil-wielding "students" who have made short work of the kitchen staff's eggs and waffles and are now engaged in feeding their minds.

TASK's adult education program was established in the late 1980s as a cornerstone of the organization's mission to provide multiple dimensions of community service, to avoid becoming, in the words of one early volunteer, simply "a monument to hunger." Staffed by a core of volunteer tutors, mainly a mix of retirees and college students, the program offers a wide range of literacy and other practical academic skills to people who, now in their 20s, 30s, 40s, even a few 50-somethings, long ago failed—or were failed by—public education. In addition to individual instruction and counseling, TASK provides all necessary supplies, from paper and pencils to work books, and will even spring for the $25 registration fee to take the state exam for a high school Graduate Equivalency Diploma (GED). "It's part of the whole concept of TASK—helping people attain self-sufficiency," says Kelly Hansen, the program's director. "And we have the same policy with an open door that we do with food. Anyone who comes here comes for free."

One thing the organization does not guarantee is that the program will be an easy ride for anyone serious about going the distance. And for most, it is not. In her previous career as a suburban high school teacher and guidance counselor, Kelly saw plenty of remedial and special-needs cases, but nothing on this scale. "A lot of my students here can't write a complete sentence," she says. One-quarter are classified as beginning readers, meaning they are functionally illiterate. Others can read, but can't write or do basic arithmetic. The drop-out rate is high, and low self-image is all but epidemic. "I can't tell you how many people come in here and when they're asked to describe themselves they tell me, 'I'm slow.' I ask, 'Why do you say that?' And they say, 'Because that's what I was always told in school.' So they learned to hate school. You ask them what kinds of jobs they see themselves in and they say things like janitor or custodian. You wonder if they were ever encouraged to dream." Which is why the achievement of even a single GED—let alone the average of six earned by TASK adult education students every year—is cause for celebration.

Seated nearby, a tall burly man who calls himself Curtis plans to follow that example soon. A 40-year-old recovering drug addict who started hitting the books at TASK almost a year ago, he recently had his first go at the GED exam and fell a few points shy of a passing grade in the math and creative writing sections. He vows it won't happen again. He wants to go on to college to become certified as a social worker or counselor—"something like that. I've been through a lot, and maybe I can help somebody else out." And he's growing impatient with himself. "I've got three brothers and three sisters, and I'm the only one got no career. But it's not too late."

At an adjoining table, Lisa has just settled into her second week in the program. Math and English workbooks stacked neatly to one side, she describes six months on streets of New Brunswick and Trenton where she "wandered around, slept in abandoned buildings. I didn't have a job, couldn't keep any money." Picked up by the authorities and diagnosed with an out-of-control bipolar disorder, she spent several months in a psychiatric hospital before being placed in a local group home for young women. At 35, she wants a GED as the ticket to college for a nursing degree. "I had to get on my feet," she says. "This is something I've got to do. I can't go around for the rest of my life with no education."

•   •   •

It's after ten now, and today's volunteer contingent (everyone showed up as expected, so no need for Plan B) is assembled at the edge of the kitchen for a final briefing. They are reminded to smile and told it's time to suit up—plastic full-length aprons and gloves for all, hair nets for the women, and for the men, white paper caps that make you look like you work at what used to be called a soda fountain. Sheepish at the prospect of donning this costume, a couple of the Lawrenceville kids horse around but shrug it off with mumbled jokes as they head off to their assignment—bagging cookies, crackers and other items in the rear pantry. Other volunteers draw duty on the serving line out front. As they move to their assigned places, one wide-eyed man in the group, an obvious neophyte, is still fussing with an apron. He is a retired hospital executive, and he readily acknowledges a tenderfoot status at TASK. "I've always been a 'big picture' kind of guy," he says, "always focused on policy, that kind of stuff. You know, write a check and solve the problem." He credits his wife, who has been volunteering for years with a church group, with "opening my eyes" to the immediate need. "She said, 'This is where it starts. Why don't you just put the gloves on and do something right now?'"

•   •   •

At precisely 10:30, the front doors swing open, and the first arrivals stream inside, mostly men, a disheveled but orderly lot that's been gathering out on the sidewalk for the last half hour or so. While some stake out familiar territory among the numbered dining tables, others make a beeline for a set of chairs lining the wall near Cathy Vandegrift's office. This is coveted real estate: occupants of these seats will be first in line to receive one of TASK's most prized offerings—packets of soap, toothpaste and brush, deodorant, a razor and a small bottle of shampoo. These "hygiene bags" are distributed sparingly, one per patron every 30 days, because supplies, heavily reliant on donations, are limited. But the underground economy is a factor, too. The contents of these pouches, which often include high-end mini-bars of soap and bottles of shampoo "donated" by hotel bathrooms and passed along to TASK by people who travel a lot, carry a collective street value of up to five dollars apiece and have been known to figure as currency in the illicit drug market.

As the tables fill amid a crescendo of bustle and chatter, the dining area's sound system comes alive in a deep baritone—the voice of Sam the floor manager. Microphone in hand, he throws out a general welcome, thanks the volunteer groups and makes a few cursory announcements before turning to his primary duty: traffic control. To maintain a serving line of reasonable length and speed, the tables are called in sequence with Sam positioned so every patron must pass him on the way to the food. Each is handed a ticket good for one meal; pregnant women receive two. For those with proof of employment, there are special tickets for "express" service so they don't have to risk overstaying their allotted lunch break. Having performed this drill daily for several years, Sam speaks with some authority when he says he's noticed an uptick in the ranks of the "working poor" at TASK. "You see them from minimum-wage jobs—janitor services, day laborers, junkyard workers, that sort of thing," he says. "I've also seen an increase in the number of white folks coming here. A couple of months ago, there was a young lady come in here from Hamilton (a Trenton suburb). There was a fire in her house, and her husband couldn't get out and was killed." Exactly what happened in the aftermath, whether there was an insurance gap or some other complication, Sam doesn't know. But "she's one of our patrons now," he says. "She told me, 'I have nothing.' You would never think a person like that would end up here." He shakes his head and goes on handing out tickets.

The line moves along smoothly, until the first stop: an array of desserts—iced and powdered donuts, cookies, cupcakes, fruit pastries, occasionally (depending on what arrives courtesy of local stores and bakeries) slices of pie and cake. People tend to linger here, TASK staffers say, not just because the spread looks inviting but because it offers an intangible bonus typically beyond the reach of these consumers: the power of choice, however fleeting. A volunteer hands over the dessert selection, and others set about filling rectangular foam-plastic plates, the kind with separate compartments, with salad, fruit, spaghetti and a roll. A large cup of juice rounds out the meal, and each patron is given a set of plastic flatware wrapped in a napkin, along with a few packets of salt and pepper—usually the last stop. But today, there are two more on the circuit: a soup station and, beyond that, a hand-truck stacked with boxes of bottled juice—bounty from that call to the kitchen an hour or so ago heralding an unsolicited delivery. The man distributing the juice, two to a customer, is none other than the kitchen supervisor himself, and patrons at a nearby table, noting Sam's presence on the crowded floor, burst into laughter as a boisterous man in jeans and a black sweater cracks wise with the architect of today's meal.

"Hey, Sam," he shouts, "looks like you did a helluva job with this sauce. But I haven't tasted it yet, and I'm a helluva food critic." Moments later, his review, delivered with a grin: "Yeah, it's fine."

Among the kaleidoscope of faces that now fill the room—black, brown, white, bearded, smiling, grimacing, staring, vacant—the mood runs the gamut. Some people obviously know each other and engage in animated conversation. Some stare at their trays. Some just sit and watch. But there is one common denominator, and it is palpable: a sense of wariness, of being on guard. It's in their eyes. So is weariness. At table number six, a man who calls himself Michael is eating and fuming over a snafu he says has thrown a wrench into his efforts to obtain necessary medication. "I'm 47. I've had two heart attacks and take seven different medicines, and now they're telling me I got to go all the way to Camden to a medical center," he says, reaching into a pocket and pulling out a plastic bag stuffed with prescriptions. Across from him, a glassy-eyed woman puts her tray down, takes a seat and pokes at the spaghetti, complaining of a headache that won't go away. She says she's waiting to get into a drug rehabilitation program, maybe in a week or two. Lately, she's been spending nights in a shelter at the Rescue Mission of Trenton. "Beats being out on the street," she says. She declines to offer a name, as does a man at the other end of the table who says his preferred nighttime venue is neither the streets nor the Rescue Mission. "I sleep under a bridge," he says matter-of-factly, "have for about three years. Every now and then the police run me off, but I just go further down the river for a week or so." He used to drive trucks for a living but fell into trouble with alcohol. "The Lord," he says, "took the craving away" a decade and a half ago. Asked how he got into his current predicament, he shrugs. Asked why he comes to the soup kitchen, he resists the temptation, if he has it, to answer a stupid question in kind. He simply says, "It's got good food, and it keeps me alive."

•   •   •

Pay close attention to the rhythms and movements of this place, and you notice a steady stream of people, one by one, entering and exiting a small cubicle in one corner of the dining area. Some stay inside for a few minutes, others far longer. It goes on all through lunch. This nook has a door with a window, and if you look inside, you can see them conferring with a woman whose desk is covered with stacks of papers and file folders. She is a social worker, one of two who serve at TASK under a contract with Catholic Charities. Mary Ann Dobson, who works with a colleague, Anne Hamilton, has the duty today and so far, half a dozen current and would-be clients have crossed her tiny threshold looking for help with problems that range from the mundane to the tangled to the truly catastrophic.

In the latter category, one young man with a crushed expression sat down a few minutes ago and told her he had just gotten the results of a blood test showing he is infected with the virus that causes AIDS. "He was very upset, and we talked for a while. He wanted someone to talk to, and that's fine," she says. In terms of an active response, all she could do at the moment was refer him to a local public health clinic where counselors could talk to him about living with the disease. On average, three AIDS cases walk through her door every month.

Dobson picks up another file and proceeds to describe an ugly battle brewing over the rights to an unborn child due within weeks. The story unravels like a bad dream. The mother, addicted to crack cocaine, already has three children in foster care through the state's child-welfare agency, the Division of Youth and Family Services (DYFS). This morning, a man claiming responsibility for the latest pregnancy asked how to go about a getting DNA test to establish custody. As a child, he was himself thrust into foster care. Now 22, he is unemployed. To make matters worse, he has a criminal record and no permanent place to live. "He wants the baby because he thinks it's his," Dobson says, "but there are a lot of questions. Even if he does [get custody] and finds housing, how is he going to keep that housing? He doesn't have any parenting skills, and who's going to care for the child if he gets a job? Plus, how do you withstand the added pressure of having a child possibly born with an addiction? If you've ever seen a child born with an addiction, it's not a pretty sight." His response to this barrage of harrowing issues, she says, plainly indicated that few of them had even occurred to him. But he walked out determined to pursue the case, the ragged outline of which is drearily familiar. "We have many young men coming in here whose children are in DYFS who want to get their kids," she says, "but they don't know how to handle the situation." For that reason, it has occurred to her more than once that TASK, at the very least, should boost its service menu with classes in parenting skills.

Another familiar phenomenon took a seat before Dobson in the form of a young woman who has been struggling to find a job in the weeks since her release from prison. During the last few days, it seems, she has met with some success. An interview led to an offer—but there's a catch: the job is in Pennington, a small town about 10 miles north of Trenton. She has no car and no cash to cover bus fare back and forth for the two weeks it will take to earn an initial paycheck. "Part of her parole requirement is to be employed," says Dobson. "Otherwise, she goes back to prison to serve the rest of her term." This is not an uncommon scenario. Indeed, in the worst of such post-prison obstacle courses, the TASK case workers have seen individuals incarcerated for 15 years or more abruptly released, in effect "dropped off in the center of Trenton," with little recourse other than to make their way to the Rescue Mission or the soup kitchen. The woman's file, an ink and paperwork quilt of phone contacts, scribbled notes and unresolved questions, joins others in a stack—the bureaucratic trappings of lives in crisis, what social workers mean by the term "caseload." Dobson looks it over and offers a sort of extemporaneous epistle, equal parts hope and resignation. "I believe most people are essentially good," she says. "If given a little opportunity, I really believe they could pick themselves up. But often because of their past, especially if they have a criminal record, it's a vicious cycle. They can't get a job, and because they can't get a job, they're stuck in the past. They can't move forward."

•   •   •

Early afternoon, and a lull has settled over the soup kitchen. The lunch crowd has given way to a scattering of latecomers who knock at the door for a limited supply of foil-wrapped leftovers. Mike Mendez, push-broom at the ready, attends to the post-meal clutter, cleaning and arranging tables for the afternoon session of adult education. Other staffers take seats to grab a bite. Off to one side, in what passes here for the executive suite—another cubbyhole of an office—the man responsible for running TASK on a daily basis takes advantage of this break in the action to sort through his own caseload, a thorny assortment of administrative and operational matters that go to the health and welfare of the organization itself.

Looming large at the moment on Peter Wise's radar screen is the construction of an approximately 3,500-square-foot addition to TASK's physical plant for food storage and preparation, patron services and plain old elbow room. Years in the making, the project was deemed vital by the soup kitchen's governing board in 2001 after it became apparent that unless proper steps were taken, dwindling space one day would force drastic and unacceptable measures, including the turning away of food, clothing, supplies and, quite possibly, even hungry people. So the board had little choice but to embark on what turned out to be a long and difficult process, longer and far more difficult that anyone anticipated, stalled repeatedly by wrangling and confusion over land acquisition, design and city permitting issues. It hasn't been cheap, either. When the final bills roll in, the cost will easily top $1 million, a portion underwritten by the state but most of it provided by individual and corporate donors. Wise was intimately involved in this enterprise from the start and has been one of its biggest boosters. But at the same time, he is deeply conflicted, and he speaks for others when he expresses mixed emotions about the project's implications.

"It is certainly reassuring that the surrounding community has stepped up in terms of providing the funding," he says. "And I feel good about the fact that the majority of patrons who come here seem to feel good about what we do, and we can do more."

But it is also a reflection of the fact that the need is growing larger, not smaller; that the number of meals served at TASK is escalating at a rate approaching 10 percent a month over the same period a year ago; that the time soon will come when the organization's total annual meal count will exceed 200,000. "Why is the soup kitchen a growth industry?" Wise asks. "This is a lens through which to see we're not doing well as a society, and a stark example of how we're addressing poverty in this country. That's why I feel bad that we have to expand this place because it means that, as a society, we're going in the wrong direction."

Wise has served in TASK's top staff position for more than eight years, longer than any of his predecessors in the organization's quarter-century history—indeed, long enough now to have him fighting a pitched battle almost weekly with an unavoidable occupational hazard in this intense line of work: the phenomenon known as burn-out. As a result, he's thinking seriously these days about whether it's time to retire. Actually, it would be his second retirement, the first, in effect, having come in the late 90s when he left the corporate world. A 2006 magazine article presented an eloquent summary of how and why he was then inspired to join a struggling nonprofit rather than cash it all in under the Florida sun:

> *At first glance ... Peter Wise would appear to be an unlikely candidate to be running a soup kitchen. He has a degree in math and physics and spent a long career in the aerospace industry making weather, communications, and scientific satellites as well as components for moon missions while living in the neat and tidy eighteenth-century village of Cranbury. Twenty years ago, in the middle of his career, a friend invited him to come down to Trenton to volunteer at a Saturday soup kitchen known as Loaves and Fishes, which was run out of a church.*
>
> *"I'm a white guy from the suburbs," he says. "What am I doing Saturday morning? I'm mowing the grass, playing tennis, whatever. But this friend twisted my arm, so I went."*
>
> *In that environment, he saw, heard, smelled things he had never seen, heard, or smelled before. He was in a room filled with street people and he was depressed and turned off.*
>
> *"We rode back to Cranbury; I had done my friend a favor, I'd been there, done that—that was it,' he says. "I do not know what happened in the next couple of weeks, but I did not have what I would call a 'Shazam moment,' or what in theological terms might be called an epiphany. I did not even have what's sometimes called the small still voice in the night, the whisper in the ear. Or if I did, I didn't hear it"*
>
> *Nevertheless, a couple of weeks later he found himself back in Trenton at Loaves and Fishes. This time he saw that these people were basically no different from him. "Once I was able to see behind the façade, it made all the difference," Wise says. "I am grateful that I have never lost that feeling twenty years later."*

During Wise's tenure, the organization's budget has quadrupled to more than $1.6 million, the staff has grown, and services have been added across the board—all made possible by aggressive fund-raising. But this growth has brought new and vexing challenges, not the least of which is how to sustain the momentum while maintaining an optimal balance between spending now and reserving for the future. At the moment, TASK's financial accounts are flush. The past winter's holiday fund-raising season set new records, and the organization should be able to swallow the cost of the building project and still entertain modest program initiatives. But the expense side nonetheless is under constant assault from cost-drivers of the sort that plague any small business, with employee health insurance premiums leading the way. Further, as anyone familiar with the nonprofit world can attest, charitable giving has limits. When donations shriveled with the post-9/11 stock market collapse in 2001–02, TASK's board was left with little choice but to unsheathe a fiscal knife; among the items left on the cutting room floor that year: one full evening meal a week. Those cuts have since been restored, but memory of that unpleasant business lingers. Competition is a factor, too. Many worthy causes are in the hunt for limited dollars, and there is the ever-present prospect of a sudden diversion of public generosity toward relief from hurricanes, floods, famine, war and other natural and man-made disasters. Besides keeping an eye on the budget, Wise has spent a good deal of time working with key staffers and board members to equip the soup kitchen with a state-of-the-art accounting system to manage the growth and strengthen due diligence. Just this morning, he met with finance personnel to hash over strategies for putting the latest piece of this bookkeeping and database apparatus in place.

If there is one encouraging constant in the soup kitchen's financial matrix, it is the fact that only a small percentage of money taken in by the organization, less than 20 percent overall, goes toward administrative and fund-raising costs. The bulk winds up in the service of those "out there on the floor," as Wise puts it, where everything TASK stands for is put to the test daily under difficult and demanding circumstances.

Lately, the challenge posed by one such set of circumstances has been giving him fits—how best to minimize threats to people and property. Security problems pretty much come with the territory in this venue. Take a population already stressed in general, throw in a mix of dysfunction ranging from mental illness to drug abuse, and occasional outbursts of unruly, inappropriate and threatening behavior are bound to result. Like his top deputy, Cathy Vandegrift, Wise has had to wade into the middle of more patron confrontations than he cares to remember, and TASK has suffered its share of petty theft and vandalism. In one of the more illustrious incidents, several homeless people a few summers ago actually tapped into the soup kitchen's electrical supply via a utility pole out front and set up a sort of open-air den complete with a salvaged, jerry-wired television. Luckily, no one was hurt before they were discovered and dispersed. In 2003, after much debate punctuated by a rash of car break-ins, TASK's board decided it was time to act. Off-duty Trenton police officers, armed and in uniform, were hired to stand watch during meals. Typically, one cop per shift occupies a desk tucked discreetly but obviously at the rear of the dining area. Their presence has had a markedly stabilizing effect.

Nonetheless, serious concerns linger. Like many cities, Trenton is grappling with escalating gang and drug violence, and experienced staffers say a dissonant tone has drifted inside along with the growing numbers of patrons. Some are on edge to the point where they regularly refuse the offer of donated clothing for fear that the color—in particular red, blue or gold, which are the adopted colors of various gangs—could cause them to be taken for members of rival factions in certain neighborhoods. Cathy Vandegrift says she has actually heard patrons turn away from various items, "saying things like, 'I'd get killed wearing that hat.'" It's a sensitive, difficult issue and not just from the standpoint of patron safety. Given TASK's heavy reliance on volunteers, the organization needs to develop creative security strategies that will be effective but not draconian. "There clearly needs to be a balance here," Wise says. "We certainly don't want to scare people away."

•   •   •

With a thud, Sam Johnson drops a large plastic bin onto the stainless steel prep table and goes to work sorting through its contents, a veritable rainbow of fresh produce—green, yellow and red peppers, miniature summer squash and more. Holding up a bundle of shitake mushrooms, he laughs, "Some of this stuff, I couldn't afford to buy in the supermarket." Just delivered by TASK's van as part of a regular batch donated by a local Whole Foods outlet, these select vegetables will provide a side dish, along with potatoes, for the evening meal (which, to be perfectly technical, isn't really an evening meal but a late-afternoon supper served between 3:30 and 5:30.) The main course, turkey with gravy, has been delegated to one of Sam's top kitchen lieutenants, a muscular fellow who goes by the name of Tony and who already is ladling the dinner into deep pans, which he covers and places in the oven. Though a lighter-than-lunch turnout is expected, Tony is also responsible during this shift for shipping about 120 meals to a satellite operation across town in Trenton's South Ward. Organized in 2003 in conjunction with the First Baptist Church and dubbed the "South Trenton Soup Kitchen," it is the first experimental beachhead established elsewhere in the city under TASK's auspices. Though TASK provides the food and lends staff assistance, the long-term objective is to make the "STSK" locally self-sufficient.

For his part, Tony is a walking emblem of TASK's leg-up approach to self-sufficiency. He came to TASK in 2002 at 34, a time in his life that he once dreamed would have him positioned at the peak of a successful sports career. Growing up in a gritty blue-collar community just across the Delaware River a few miles from here, he was a stand-out athlete, a star running back and free safety on the high school football team and a talented point guard in basketball. In the mid-80s, when his team mounted a storied campaign to two consecutive state basketball titles, he was in the thick of it. College recruiters swarmed him; ultimately, he accepted a full athletic scholarship. But there was a dark side to this promising young man. In the spring of his college senior year, just before graduation, he was arrested for the armed robbery of a jewelry store. Convicted and sentenced to12 years in prison, he served every day of it as a consequence of tough new mandatory sentencing laws.

Looking back, Tony says the only way he could deal with that experience was to move forward. "Doing time like that you have to grow up very fast," he says. "I learned the importance of life, and I started to understand who I am." He also learned there are no guarantees, learned, as he puts it, that "there is never a promise that the door will ever open again." And he learned a trade. Assigned to the prison kitchen, Tony became skilled in the use of large commercial equipment and in dealing with the technical and logistical challenges that come with preparing meals for large numbers of people, skills he brought to the soup kitchen. At TASK's expense, he enrolled in an evening culinary arts program at Mercer County Community College and thoroughly applied himself, piling up 3.9 grade-point average toward a chef's apprentice certificate. Now, his eye is on a more ambitious prize: a master's degree in hospitality management. Meanwhile, he stays in shape playing semi-pro ball, and he's launched a little side venture, a sort of one-man "scared straight" program offering himself as a motivational speaker for local schools and youth groups. He sees the soup kitchen as "a stepping stone to get back into society. TASK didn't have to do this for me. They could have used the money for something else. I'm not going be here forever, but I feel I've got to set a pattern. If I don't do my part, that would be like smacking everybody in the face. They'd say, 'Why give the next guy an opportunity?'"

As Tony and several volunteers wrap meals and put them into insulated transport bins that are hand-trucked to TASK's waiting van, the assembly line out front in the dining area starts to hit its stride once again. Some familiar faces from lunch stand waiting for trays, but for the most part, it is a smaller, more subdued group, more women, a scattering of children. Near the entrance, a few patrons peel off before reaching the dining area and take a detour to their immediate right through doorway into TASK's computer room, a popular venue this time of day. Here, they have free access to the Internet, to e-mail and job-search databases, to resume preparation guides, printers, a copier and a small library of how-to books and technical manuals. On one wall, a blow-up photo of Albert Einstein gazes across at a large map of the U.S. Another poster says simply, "Thinking: It's a Habit." At one terminal in the corner, a man is watching music videos. Another is typing something in Spanish. One enterprising fellow has just printed a batch of business cards. Diane Subber, who monitors the room and teaches a variety of classes in computer skills, is seated next to a middle-aged man who has asked for help navigating a website maintained by the Virginia Bureau of Prisons. "He was looking for his son," she later explains. "They haven't seen each other in ten years, but somebody told him [the father] that he saw someone resembling his son in one of the prisons down there. This is the kind of thing some of these people are up against—trying to find friends and family. It happens frequently."

Abruptly, a commotion rattles the air. The front doors burst open and two paramedics rush in, heading in the direction of a table where a woman appears to be gasping for air. As neighboring diners move to the side, the emergency crew administers oxygen, determines she is able to walk and slowly leads her outside to an ambulance. Erwin Elsey, an off-duty city police detective providing today's soup kitchen security, says it doesn't look to be anything serious, apparently an asthma attack. An approachable, easy-going police department veteran, Elsey is one of the organizers of the off-duty coverage for TASK. He secured the go-ahead from higher-ups, enlisted available colleagues and worked with the staff to establish a schedule. Having grown up in a neighborhood nearby, Elsey routinely recognizes faces here, and that has tempered his approach to maintaining control. "For the most part, you can talk to people and de-escalate things," he says. "I'm a firm believer that if you talk to people the way you would want them to talk to you, you won't have a problem." So far, today at least, things have gone smoothly, and he's been a man of few words.

·   ·   ·

Twenty past five, and supper is winding down. The last of the donated juice is being pulled from boxes and distributed by volunteers. In the kitchen, Tony and others are wiping down the ovens and tables, sweeping up scraps, mopping every square inch of floor space. Sam Johnson wheels a cart of late trays out into the dining area and steps back for a moment to tally the day's meal count: about 350 for lunch, another 200 or so for supper; add the south Trenton shipment for a total above 600. Seated nearby, listening to this calculus, Sam the floor manager quips, "A lot of meals go through this operation—and that's on a slow day."

The front door opens, and a couple, a man and a woman, thirtyish, step in from the dimming twilight. The woman's face, badly bruised, is a swollen mask of black eyes and cuts that haven't fully healed, and as they approach, several TASK workers ask if she is all right, if she needs help. She says, "No thanks, "I'm okay, I was in a car accident the other day." The man says nothing. Handed two of the late trays, they leave.

The lights in the kitchen are turned off. Most of the staffers have left. Those who remain are packing up, putting on jackets and sweaters. Someone walks past Mike Mendez as he stacks the last of the chairs and says, "See you tomorrow, Mike—until the next episode."

2

Filling the Bowl, Finding a Home

The Trenton Area Soup Kitchen occupies a one-story metal-frame structure at the foot of a dead-end street in one of Trenton's old industrial zones, a section in the north end of town formerly known as Coalport. The building is flanked on the left by several fenced-in acres of what used to be a rail yard, now overgrown with weeds and piled with debris in the shadow of a decrepit factory. To the immediate right is the City of Trenton Animal Shelter. When cars pull in to drop off donations, supplies or volunteers at the soup kitchen, the shelter sometimes erupts in a chorus of barking and howling. Directly across Escher Street is the city's school-bus maintenance garage and beyond that a huge parking lot for the city's police headquarters. If you were to set up a small step-ladder on the sidewalk and climb up two or three rungs to gain an unobstructed view to the west, you would see the top floors of office buildings downtown with the glowing golden dome of the State Capitol smack in the middle less than a mile distant. In the opposite direction, traffic rushing north and south along Route 1 about a half-mile away fills the air with a dull roar. There are no houses in sight, no schools, no stores, no gas stations, not even a pay phone. All in all, it has the vacant feel of an old industrial park—except for this: on any given weekday starting around 10 o'clock in the morning, the drab surroundings incongruously come alive with people, hungry people, coming on foot from every direction.

How TASK came to be—and, in particular, how it came to be located in this sort of place—is a story of compassion and caring tempered by desperation, tenacity, fear, politics and compromise.

•   •   •

First, a bit about the city whose name it bears.

Situated within five miles of New Jersey's geographic center, Trenton occupies a low sloping plateau along the Delaware River just above the point where, as any map will show, a protruding triangle of southeastern Pennsylvania thrusts forth to give its foot-shaped neighbor a kick to the ankle. Locally, the city is considered part of Central Jersey, but given its very location almost in the middle of the 100-odd miles separating New York and Philadelphia, Trenton constantly feels the North Jersey/South Jersey tug of both major metropolitan areas. Hence, the galvanic admixture of things like professional sports rivalries, Eagles versus Giants in football, Phillies and Yankees in baseball, although the edge in fan loyalty involving the latter would seem to go to New York considering the presence of a Double-A minor league team affiliated with the Bronx Bombers. (Okay, in the interests of fairness and accuracy, it should be pointed out that this same franchise, the Trenton Thunder, once fed the Boston Red Sox farm system, too.)

Until the last quarter of the 17th Century, though, it was the Indians who prevailed here, an Algonquin affiliate known as the Leni-Lenape who found an abundant source of food—freshwater fish, clams and mussels—in the shallow, rock-strewn rapids of what was then known as the "Falls of the Delaware." Though unnavigable at this point except by canoe or other small craft, the swiftly moving river also held a certain appeal to the increasing numbers of European visitors who were beginning to stream into the area. Around 1679, a group of English Quakers established a settlement anchored by Mahlon Stacey's water-powered grist mill. Three decades later, a wealthy Philadelphia merchant, William Trent, became the leading landholder, and in an early reflection of how things never change, his wealth garnered naming rights as well.

Trent Towne—shortened to a single two-syllable word in 1721—was on the map.

For the next 50 years, Trenton served essentially as little more than a commercial conduit for merchants, couriers and grandees shuttling between the two burgeoning urban colonial centers north and south, a phenomenon defined by Benjamin Franklin's wry description of New Jersey as "a beer barrel tapped at both ends," or something to that effect. But in December 1776, geography conspired with fate and circumstance to give this riverine waystation a distinguished place in history. On Christmas night that year, the tattered remnants of the Continental Army, routed from New York and chased for days across open country, stood shivering in sleet and freezing rain on the Pennsylvania side of the Delaware as their leader, General George Washington, contemplated retreat or surrender—and then decided against all odds to attack. Crossing the icy river in darkness at a place called McConkey's Ferry about seven miles north of Trenton, Washington led some 1,000 troops and irregulars in a morning raid that caught the town's Hessian occupiers largely by surprise. Several days later, in an even more brazen display of tactical guile, Washington's men seized high ground on the south end of town and thwarted repeated attempts by the enemy to cross a bridge over the Assunpink Creek at the foot of Queen Street (now Broad) and link up with reinforcements heading north from Philadelphia. Then, after midnight on January 3, 1777, the Continentals left campfires burning in a decoy maneuver and slipped out of town toward Princeton where they engaged and defeated a British force dispatched from New York under the command of General Cornwallis. Historians refer to this tumultuous reversal of fortune as "the ten days" that changed the course of the war and saved the Revolution.

Oddly, the critical role played by Trenton in this turning point never found a prominent or lasting niche in the American imagination, certainly not on par with storied place-names like Lexington and Concord, Bunker Hill, Valley Forge or Yorktown. There is nothing that rivals Philadelphia's Independence Hall, no museum dedicated to the crucible events which swept the city. Indeed, only a few overt reminders are scattered about: a 55-foot-tall columned battle monument topped with a figure of Washington, a faithfully restored colonial barracks, annual "Patriots Week" reenactments and walking tours, a few weathered plaques commemorating key battle points, but little else. Long forgotten except perhaps by scholars of the period is the fact that in 1784, Trenton actually won Congress' designation as capital of the newly minted United States, a distinction that lasted all of two months. (Two decades later, it would again serve briefly as the seat of national government when a yellow fever epidemic swept Philadelphia.)

A consolation prize of sorts arrived in1789 when Trenton was officially chartered the capital of New Jersey, and for many decades thereafter, it benefited richly from a nexus of commerce, power and influence that came with occupying the center of the state's political universe in a time of burgeoning national expansion and economic growth. Just as it had served as a vital springboard in the war for national independence, Trenton helped energize the Industrial Revolution. Wrought iron beams manufactured by the Trenton Iron Co. in 1847 were used to support the dome of the U.S. Capitol. Structural steel and wire suspension cable for the Brooklyn and Golden Gate bridges were produced by the famed home-grown industrial firm of Thomas A. Roebling & Sons. The city became a national center for the production of pottery, highlighted by porcelain creations bearing renowned names like Lenox, Stangle and Boehm. Farm tools, cigars, linoleum, mattresses and more—factory after factory churned out products and shipped the goods to all points on the compass, the resulting wealth underwriting a host of local amenities: thriving retail shops, State Street mansions and landscaped greenswards, including Cadwalader Park, an oasis of trees and fields on the northwestern end of town designed by Frederick Law Olmsted, architect of none other than New York's Central Park. In 1896, the nation's first professional basketball game was played in Trenton. Two decades later, in a burst of civic pride, the city fathers commissioned production of a huge sign and hung it on the lower bridge spanning the Delaware. It featured the winning entry in a 1911 chamber of commerce slogan contest that drew more than 1,400 entries: "Trenton Makes, The World Takes."

Nearly a century later, that sign, fully refurbished in 2002, still illuminates the night, but the glowing red neon must surely be a source of puzzlement to train passengers whooshing past dilapidated buildings along the nearby Northeast Corridor line. Even for many residents of the city, it long ago took on a certain hollowness, the silent boast diminished, the message less a statement of pride than a poignant beacon of down-but-not-out defiance in the face of forces seemingly beyond the control of anyone or any entity, including the State of New Jersey itself.

The unraveling, of course, did not occur overnight. Following a pattern that came to haunt many small-and medium-sized industrial centers of the Northeast and Midwest after World War II, the local wealth simply started to drain away into the maw of a changing economy. Factories moved or closed altogether. Jobs were lost, and so were people. Trenton's population peaked at about 135,000 in 1950, then stagnated for another decade or so before settling into a steady decline. (The 2000 Census pegged it at slightly over 85,000.) The socio-economic landscape, meanwhile, acquired the aspect of a distinct racial divide. With suburban development spreading outward in every direction, white residents in rising numbers flocked across the city limits to reside in new homes, attend new schools, shop in new strip malls. The declining urban venue they left behind became, in turn, an island of affordability that drew upon the postwar migration of southern blacks in search of opportunity. In all too many instances, though, these new Trentonians wound up instead mired in a morass of low wages, unemployment and substandard housing, and by the mid-60s, the handwriting was on the wall: beyond the greenswards and limestone edifices of state government, Trenton was becoming defined as a core of want surrounded by an ever-widening circle of plenty. Local political leaders, civic groups and urban renewal experts worked to reverse course, but they were overtaken by events that crippled the city's long-term effort to reinvent itself.

The first major blow came in April 1968 when, in a shattering echo of the racial unrest that convulsed urban American with the murder of civil rights leader Dr. Martin Luther King, Trenton saw its downtown torn apart by a days-long rampage of looting, ransacking and arson. Some of the worst violence occurred right in the shadow of the Washington Battle Monument. Before the rioting ended, one person lay dead, scores were injured and more than 300 people, mostly young black males, were under arrest. Business losses exceeded $7 million, and insurers abruptly cut their own losses and bailed out of plans to underwrite further redevelopment. In the final analysis, the riots served as a primary catalyst for abandonment of the city's once-thriving retail district by longtime anchor stores, including fancy jewelry purveyors like Lippman's, popular furniture outlets like Convery's, sporting-goods shops like Snyder's and large, well-stocked department stores like Dunham's, Goldberg's and Nevius Voorhees. Twelve years later, its resilience further worn by the energy-price-driven economic turmoil of the 70s, the city experienced a kind of *coup de grace* as the worst recession since the Great Depression swept the nation. "That really hit Trenton hard," recalls one survivor of the downturn's sky-high interest rates and ballooning unemployment. "It was sort of the last bang of the industrial era going out with a whimper. Lots of people lost jobs, and for the poor who were just hanging on, it was very hard."

•   •   •

Among those who bucked the trend and actually moved into the city during this era was a Presbyterian minister returning to the U.S. after extensive missionary work abroad. The Rev. Arthur L. Stanley had spent six years serving as chaplain of a school in Seoul, South Korea, along with his wife Barbara, who was a teacher, and their two children. As 1978 dawned, his overseas contract was expiring and, as he evaluated various options, he decided to accept a one-year transitional assignment raising church funds in New Jersey. Working from a base in the state capital, Stanley took advantage of the opportunity to range widely in and around Trenton, meeting fellow pastors, getting to know the place, the people, their circumstances. Something about the city captivated him from the start. "I was born in 1926 and grew up in the Depression years," he says. "My dad didn't have a very important job; he worked for the highway department in Washington, D.C. building roads, and we really struggled." When he was five years old, Stanley's parents were forced to sell their home in Silver Spring, Md. "We wound up in a place called 'tar paper alley' with six or eight other families back in a dirt road where we just kind of built places that would give some shelter. We didn't have much, and I think that always gave me an orientation for social services." Which is why, in 1979, when the temporary fund-raising work came to an end and two offers of extended service arose—either leading a small community congregation near rural State College, Pa., or running a council of churches in Trenton—Stanley was not entirely surprised by the ease of his choice. "For sure, we could have been up in the quiet of the mountains and all that good stuff," he says, "but I really felt drawn to the inner city for the opportunity of that challenge, and when the offer was made, I felt called to accept it."

Stanley's dual position as both pastor of Bethany Presbyterian Church and head of the Trenton Ecumenical Area Ministry, known as TEAM, gave him a unique platform for learning about the city's troubles. Settling into a rented house just off Greenwood Avenue, it quickly became apparent that his new quarters virtually straddled one of the more notable cultural demarcations in the Trenton social grid, bounded on one side by predominantly black neighborhoods and on the other by the outer edges of a long-established Italian working-class section known as Chambersburg. "There'd been some racial conflict in the area," he recalls, "and we became aware not only of those concerns but also of serious problems with housing. And that led me to wonder about the problem of hunger. One thing that stood out in particular was that we would get a lot of people showing up at our church door every day and every night who were hungry and looking for food."

In conversations with others around town, the Stanleys heard the same phenomenon described again and again, especially by fellow clergy: people turning up at all hours asking for something to eat. Meetings of TEAM representatives were convened, and as they started piecing together a broader profile of need, one particularly stark aspect loomed large: the sheer absence in most parts of the city of any place to buy basic supplies of food. "There were simply no grocery stores left downtown," Stanley recalls. "People were having to walk or ride buses out to the suburbs to do any shopping." That gap in particular became a key touchstone as the group mulled various relief strategies. Eventually, the idea was hatched to establish a food cooperative, a place where people could at least obtain staples—beans, rice, canned goods and other non-perishables—conveniently and at little or no cost.

As the discussions gained momentum, however, it became apparent that a certain level of local logistical expertise would be required if there was to be any realistic hope of getting the thing up and running. Stanley found that know-how in the person of Alice Parker. A nurse by training, Parker was the kind of person who didn't seem to appreciate that there were limited hours in the day, and much of her free time was devoted to volunteer social work. Between hospital shifts in Philadelphia, she worked on shelter programs for Trenton's homeless women and children. She also took it upon herself to solicit and distribute batches of donated food. "I was always going into Philadelphia to pick up bread, muffins, whatever," she says. "Every Friday, we would come back and give out muffins, just stand on the street corners and give out muffins." Parker also possessed a wealth of helpful connections to Trenton's nonprofit social-welfare infrastructure. She was deeply involved with the Trenton chapter of the Volunteers of America and had extensive ties to other organizations, such as the Forum Project, a Hanover Street agency that sought ways to help ex-offenders become productive members of the community. In the fall of 1980, its central downtown location seemed a perfect venue for the nascent food co-op.

"There was always a need for food, for clothing, for shelter," Parker says, "and I met with Art, and we talked about what we were going to do. I was the one who was available to do the 'hands-on' stuff. My job was to find a facility where we could feed people. We didn't know how.

We had no budget. We had no money. But we had a concept, and I always felt God was on my side."

As it turned, God evidently took the long view. Despite its ease of accessibility and an initially well-stocked array of canned food and bagged dry goods, the co-op never got off the ground. Where heavy demand was expected, only a trickle of takers showed up. What's more, it soon became painfully obvious to the organizers that a co-op system was of little use to community's neediest—the homeless—because they had no means to prepare raw food. There were other factors, too. "We just didn't have the foundation or the backing or the resources to make it go," Art Stanley says. "It didn't last very long, but it certainly opened up our awareness of the need."

Back at the drawing board, the Stanleys and Parker changed focus, honing in on how to go about establishing a place where actual meals could be cooked, served and consumed on a regular basis. They also broadened the circle of volunteer involvement. Beginning in the summer of 1981, individuals from a score of organizations were invited to brainstorming sessions. People like Rev. John Nelson, pastor of Trenton's First Presbyterian Church; Rev. John Weatherly, rector of Christ Episcopal Church; Terese Vogel, First Presbyterian's day-care center director; Cathy Cuffey, head of the Forum Project to help ex-offenders; and Judith Eastland of WE Inc., a Trenton-based community service group. Also, as long-term events would show—especially when it came to the need for a constantly replenished supply of volunteers—one of the group's wisest and most judicious moves was to reach beyond the city limits for help, calling on lay activists and leaders of suburban congregations in Princeton, Pennington, Hamilton and elsewhere to lend a hand. Among those drawn into the mix was a recent Princeton University graduate, Martin Johnson, who, by coincidence, was nurturing a separate organization, dubbed Isles Inc., to pursue creative, neighborhood-scale community development projects in Trenton. "It was a heady time," Johnson says, recalling the burst of grassroots initiatives and what he describes as the "yeasty," reform-minded discussions amid looming social-welfare cutbacks by the Reagan administration. "These were very important discussions to have because they involved not just the faith-based institutions and not just those who were social-service care-givers. They also involved, you know, what's the role of the public here? What's the real role of the public and of government?"

By late fall, after much back and forth, participants had developed skeletal plans to move forward with a volunteer food-service operation, but they remained uncertain over the ultimate shape and mechanics. John Nelson, one of the more impatient members of the group, recalls a critical juncture: "Eventually, the subject got around to a soup kitchen, which was something most of us had heard of, seen operating in films, but which nobody had any first-hand knowledge of. I listened, and then, in my usual brusque way at the end of the meeting, announced that I wasn't coming to any more meetings the purpose of which was to talk about things. That comment got me the job of putting together an organizational proposal for a soup kitchen. I had had ten years of teaching at a seminary where I was the person who got stuck with putting together the 'DMin' (Doctor of Ministry) professional degree program, and I knew something about organization. So I brought an organizational chart to the next meeting—and that's pretty much how I got to be chairman of the soup kitchen board the first year." Nelson was also the person who cooked up a name for the new venture. "I was simply looking for an acronym, which I always think is helpful in publicizing something," he says. "So, with 'SK' as in 'Soup Kitchen,' and 'T' as in Trenton, the only 'A' I could think of was 'Area.'" Shortly thereafter, with the requisite paperwork filed at the Secretary of State's office, New Jersey's newest nonprofit corporation was officially in business with the stated objective "to feed the truly needy people of Trenton five days a week without cost to the individual in need."

Adopting a name, an organizational structure and a goal, however, was one thing. The next step was a bit more complicated: finding a base of operations. But thanks to the resourceful Alice Parker, a solution abruptly appeared at hand. Working behind the scenes and drawing on her connections in the community, she had approached Mount Zion A.M.E. Church on Perry Street and found a receptive audience. The leadership and congregation listened to the idea and offered to host the soup kitchen in the church's finished basement. Together with TASK representatives, they negotiated a lease, and everything seemed in order—except for one rather large unanticipated catch. Upon inspection, the city refused to grant an occupancy permit absent steps to remedy a host of fire-hazard and egress issues. Given cost estimates that dwarfed TASK's meager treasury, this development was a deal killer, and despite follow-up efforts to work out a compromise, the municipal edict stood. With that, the organizers went off in search of an alternate venue—an exercise that was to become all too tediously familiar in the years to come.

At this early stage, though, luck was on their side, and a fall-back materialized in fairly short order. With the approach of winter in late 1981, word reached John Nelson that leaders of Trenton's First United Methodist Church were willing to entertain TASK's proposal. One of the city's oldest established religious institutions—regular services were already being held there several years before Washington's troops successfully defended the creek bridge just a hundred yards south on what is now called Broad Street—this venerable stone landmark presented itself as a potentially advantageous location for several reasons. Situated a half-block off State Street in the heart of downtown, the church was an obvious destination easily reached from any direction. It had a fully equipped kitchen complete with a food prep area and a basement meeting room conveniently accessible from the street and large enough to accommodate a small crowd. Better still, although a few modifications to the physical plant were necessary, they were relatively minor, and city officials readily gave the green light.

On January 13, 1982, TASK served it first meal. "I'll never forget that day," says Parker, who had stepped into what was then the unpaid role of director, cook, volunteer supervisor and meal-service manager all wrapped into one. "We didn't know how the soup kitchen was going to go, and that day, I made enough soup to feed an army." According to a brief narrative sketch of TASK's early days prepared some years ago by a volunteer, John Valentine, the inaugural event proceeded apace and without incident: "Volunteers came on duty at eleven; at one o'clock, the doors were opened and they remained open for two hours. Sixty persons altogether came. They were served turkey soup and crackers, a peanut butter sandwich, Jello and either coffee or a fruit drink. The setting for each table included a discreetly placed prayer card; in voting to approve this feature, the [TASK governing] Board respected to some degree the wishes both of those who strongly favored a public prayer of thanksgiving and those who considered such a practice intrusive if not offensive." Three weeks later, Valentine wrote, "Alice Parker submitted her first report. A total of 964 people had so far been served—589 adults, 370 seniors and 5 children. Twenty were served on the quietest day, 92 on the busiest day. She estimated that roughly fifty percent of those served were 'repeats.' During this period, she had spent a total of $285 dollars on food and supplies; most of the food and disposable supplies were donated."

Parker vividly remembers the regular drill she followed and the simple pitch she gave to corral those donations and recruit sufficient volunteers to staff the serving line every day. Working in conjunction with Barbara Stanley—who presided over the nurturing of what eventually grew into a circle of nearly two dozen dependable volunteer groups—Parker paid visits to service organizations, civic groups, labor unions and "every church in the area to get them on board. What I asked them to do was come in one day a week. I told them, 'When people come to the soup kitchen, there is no color, no creed. But they do have one thing in common. They are hungry. On the other hand, we have a choice. Before we go to bed at night, we can go into our cupboards or into our refrigerators and we can choose what we want to eat. These people are less fortunate. They don't have that luxury.' And I asked them to give, and that's how we started getting donations.

"I was begging everybody," she says. "I was the begging-est person in town, and it just took off!"

Besides gifts of money—enough to enable TASK that first year to amass a $22,000 operating budget—people turned up at the church bearing bags and boxes of food. Bakeries and suburban grocery stores joined in, notably the sprawling Pennington Market, among the first food emporiums in the area to set aside leftover produce, bread, rolls, pastries and other provisions for the soup kitchen. As word spread, other commercial outlets signed on. John Weatherly recalls one day early on when he and other volunteers drove south to Camden to redeem an offer from the Campbell Soup Co. "We hauled back a truck-load of soup, and it took us a whole day to go down, load and transport it back to one of my parishes on Brunswick Avenue. Most of the cans were missing labels. There was a code book that told you the contents of the cans, but generally we didn't need it; we just dumped them into the pot." For her part, Parker preferred to prepare the main course, when she could, the old-fashioned way—from scratch. "I went to local restaurants to get soup recipes, never did canned soup" she says. "I did a corn chowder so well they put the recipe in the newspaper."

As TASK's first anniversary rolled around amid a burst of publicity, it became readily apparent that the need was growing, not diminishing as some of the organizers had expected. "I grew up in the 30s, and I knew what soup and bread lines were and then the war came and things changed and all that stuff just went away," says Stanley. "So our thinking at the time was that we'll just be doing this for a while, that it would be some kind of temporary expedient and that things would improve and it would just go away." *The Times* of Trenton reported that more than 200 meals were served on January 13, 1983—nearly quadruple the number on opening day a year earlier and a grand total of 40,520 over the course of the initial 12 months. But the patron mix wasn't just growing; it was changing: beyond the hardcore homeless and street people, more young adults were turning up, more unemployed, more families with young children. All of which meant that the running of the place was getting more costly and more complicated.

"I ran a tight ship," says Parker, whose burgeoning workload had finally erased any lingering doubt over the need for paid full-time staff. "I didn't feed people that had been drinking. I made everybody take their hats off. I would walk downstairs and onto the floor and the hats came off. I had no cursing, no fighting. I didn't tolerate that foolishness.

I even got some of the men to stay after and help clean up in exchange for extra soup." In late 1983, the increasing floor-management responsibilities were spun off into the capable, and sizable, hands of a new staffer, Margaret Byrd, a former volunteer described by Valentine as "a grandmother with a big heart, a wide girth and a voice capable of knocking down the walls of Jericho." Those privileged to witness the peculiar crowd-control skills of this woman, known to all as "Mom" or "Big Mama," describe a combination bouncer/comforter who occupied a strategic spot at the base of stairs leading directly into the dining area. Using red, white and black poker chips to keep count of the men, women and children entering the hall, and some sort of invisible antennae to detect any trouble brewing, Byrd demonstrated an uncanny ability to keep order yet maintain a friendly, welcoming atmosphere no matter the circumstance. "She ran that dining room, no question," recalls Beverly Mills, a volunteer who showed up on the church doorstep one day to see what TASK was about. "They didn't dare say one disrespectful word to her. I had to laugh a couple of times because these people would come in, some of them off their meds, talking crazy and such, but when they got in her presence, they would straighten right up."

Mills speaks with more than casual familiarity. In 1984, she was hired to replace Alice Parker, who decided to devote full time to other charitable endeavors, notably the establishment of a shelter in Trenton for homeless women. Although Mills had no experience running an organization like TASK, her selection made sense from a number of fundamental angles: she was young and willing to work hard; she had direct links to the suburbs, starting with Pennington, her home town; and, in her volunteer visits to TASK, she was clearly taken by the spirit of the place. Though accepting the job meant juggling a busy college schedule, Mills felt it was something she needed to do. "I was never aware of any soup kitchens being around, and I'd been working in the state Public Advocate's office when a co-worker mentioned something about a food drive in the city for poor people downtown," she recalls. "So I went down there and afterwards just couldn't stop thinking about it, what I saw, the people who went there. It really got in my head."

More deeply, as subsequent events would demonstrate, than she could ever have imagined.

Mills spent nearly two years at the TASK helm, her hands full from the start. During the month she took over, August 1984, the soup kitchen served record numbers—4,138 meals in all, an average of more than 130 per day. Within a year, the annual meal count would top 50,000 for the first time. The portrait of need continued to evolve, too, as increasing numbers of elderly people came through the door looking for relief. In response, Mills organized efforts to expand the nutritional base, augmenting the regular soup menu with specials that included hamburgers and an occasional spaghetti feast. "We had to be creative," she says. "Whatever we had on hand, that's what we would build the day's meal on. For example, if we got a load of lettuce or some fruit, we'd make a huge salad." As to actual demand, there was never a day when no one showed up for food, but Mills and others did note distinct fluctuations—to this day a signature soup kitchen cycle: light at the beginning of the month, heavy toward the end when people feel the squeeze of multiple bills coming due and cash assistance running out. "In those days, they'd all be lined up out on the sidewalk an hour before we started serving," she recalls. "It could be any kind of weather, and the minute you opened up, here they'd come streaming in."

One day, as Mills surveyed the crowd, a familiar face caught her eye—and she felt her stomach jump with a shock of recognition: "I looked up, and I saw my cousin standing there."

He had been a handsome young man once, outgoing, extremely bright with an IQ that qualified him for membership in Mensa. He landed a promising position with the Exxon Corp., fell in love and married, bought a house and settled in North Jersey. "We were only one year apart [in age], and we'd been very close," she says. "We spent summers together and family meals together. I remember one time we had this huge family deal for my grandfather's 75th birthday, and we were both there."

But then it all came apart against a tide of mental illness diagnosed as schizophrenia.

"He refused treatment, and we didn't know where he was for years, didn't know if he was dead or alive, and then there he was at the soup kitchen in filthy clothing, matted hair, disheveled, like a homeless person. I went over to talk to him, but he was very angry, belligerent, and made it clear that he didn't want anything to do with me. I remember my aunt—his mother, her only child—being so happy because with me there, there would be this link, that I would see him regularly. But I also remember him telling me he would only come back to eat if I stayed away from him and didn't say a word to him." More than two decades later, Beverly Mills still feels the sting of this rebuke, and her eyes fill with tears. "And so I would see him but I wouldn't say anything.

"Then he stopped coming every day, and there was a period of time when we didn't see him come around at all and then one day—I remember it was winter and cold—my aunt got a phone call telling her he had been found dead inside someone's garage."

The experience, Mills says, taught her all she needed to know about human vulnerability and the imperative of compassion in the face of it.

"Here was someone who had a good job, a wife, the whole nine yards. You start out working in a good job and trying to build a life and then you're suddenly faced with this awful illness and you're pretty much powerless to deal with it because you don't know what's going on. How many others are there?

"You know, people can say that those who go to a soup kitchen or whatever are shiftless and could do better if they just tried. But this was someone who really didn't have a chance to do that. What about that, and what about all the others?"

•   •   •

In 1985, TASK entered its fourth year in the heart of Trenton feeling the pressure of growth from both inside and out. With annual operating costs above $57,000 and climbing, and a budgetary reserve starting to erode, organizers discovered that the early blush of fund-raising wasn't so easy to sustain. Wear-and-tear on the church's physical plant was mounting—some $5,000 had to be earmarked for maintenance during

1984 alone—and security was becoming a costly annoyance in the form of occasional overnight and weekend break-ins that left supplies pillaged and depleted.

Most ominous, though, was the deteriorating relationship between the soup kitchen and its neighbors.

Grumbles of discontent, to be sure, had been audible from day one among area merchants and restaurant owners, and for obvious reasons. From their vantage point, this new enterprise in their midst didn't just deliver charity; it also threatened to serve as a business-killing magnet for vagrants, derelicts and other unsavory characters—and right at the very time the city was struggling with the commercial viability of the so-called "Trenton Commons," a block-long stretch of State Street between Broad and Warren that had been converted into a sort of would-be pedestrian shopping mall. Angst over the soup kitchen "was always on a simmer," Mills says, recalling instances when local emotions actually boiled over. "I remember there was this one skinny little guy who would come in and scream about one thing or another. He was always outraged, very angry with the church for letting us rent space there." Exercising its political muscle, the Trenton Commons Commission, the downtown business group (forerunner of the Trenton Downtown Association), took the mounting complaints of its members to City Hall. Meanwhile, rumors flew of imminent lawsuits seeking to declare the daily activities at the church a public nuisance. "We're not opposed to the concept of a soup kitchen," one Commission official told *The Times*, "but to its location. There's panhandling and cursing and it attracts a lower element of people." In response, the city assigned more police to the area, and TASK agreed to take steps to change and control the manner in which its patrons gathered, entered and exited the church.

But it was too little, too late. The business community lobbied the city for a special committee to resolve the conflicting interests, and the panel made no secret of its favored solution: finding a way to move the soup kitchen elsewhere. For their part, TASK officials initially dug in their heels and refused to participate, a posture that only seemed to inflame matters. The tipping point came in November 1985 when

United Methodist's governing board, by formal letter, disclosed its intention to terminate the lease effective March 1 the following year.

Looking back, Cynthia Krommes, then-pastor of Trenton's St. Bartholomew's Church and chair of TASK's board during part of this tumultuous period, says the events that put the soup kitchen under threat of eviction were probably inevitable given the full brocade of circumstances in play at the time. "You have to remember that the people of United Methodist had really bent over backwards getting involved with this, which everyone thought would be temporary, but then one year went into the next and then the next and so on," she says. "And there was a lot of pressure. Poor people basically were being drawn into downtown when state workers were going out to lunch, and the business people saw it scaring away their customers. What I think finally happened was that the merchants kind of ganged up on the church board. But to be fair to the merchants, a lot of them were hard-working people, and they were barely hanging on by their fingertips, too."

As the controversy gained momentum—and generated headlines (the prospect of the soup kitchen itself becoming the latest victim of homelessness in Trenton was a juicy story line)—all eyes were drawn to the man in the middle of it all: Arthur J. Holland, the city's long-time mayor.

A veteran of the city's preeminent Democratic (and, in those days, predominantly white) power structure, Art Holland became Trenton's top elected official in 1959 and, with the exception of a four-year hiatus triggered by a Republicans surge in 1966, served almost continuously in that role until his death in 1989. He was an ex-seminarian who gravitated to politics with a progressive bent, an old-school New Deal/Great Society liberal who kept an open door, didn't mind getting into the trenches and saw government as a tool to spur economic development and promote social welfare, even when those goals got in the way of each other. Ultimately, Holland put up a mixed and incomplete record on both counts, but he tried. With Trenton at a critical juncture, he recognized the need for drastic measures and creative experimentation, and he was not shy about leading by example—starting with his own family's living arrangements.

House-hunting early in 1964 with wife Betty and infant daughter, Holland eschewed the city's remaining upscale sections in favor of a worn-out neighborhood called Mill Hill. Once an opulent clutch of Federalist and Victorian townhouses dating to the mid-1800s, this residential knoll between downtown and the train station area had long since become an emblem of decay. The Hollands, however, looked beyond the cracked and crumbling facades and envisioned something quite different: comfortable brick homes and quaint cobbled streets illuminated by gas lamps—a Georgetown-esque enclave waiting to be reborn. Eventually, of course, Mill Hill was reborn (albeit without the cobblestones), but few people at the time were willing to put money on it. The fact that the mayor himself did, buying and renovating a run-down structure there, was a potent symbol. Indeed, his investment made international news, including front-page treatment in *The New York Times*, as reporters seized on the irresistible tale of a white politician actually settling into a low-income, predominantly black neighborhood. In retrospect, given the tenor of the times—segregation, civil rights, freedom marches—the breathless coverage seems hardly surprising. But Holland shook his head in dismay over the whole florid hullabaloo. To his way of thinking, the media spectacle was "a tragedy," because if something as prosaic as this was big news, if people considered him some sort of hero—or villain, for that matter—just for moving to a certain section of the city he governed, it was another sorry reflection of the country's deep socio-economic and racial divide. No small irony, then, that in succeeding years, as he pursued his own brand of urban revitalization elsewhere is the city, Holland himself would be caught up on a rough edge of that very same divide.

People who knew or worked with him in the early 80s describe a man genuinely torn over the circumstances that put the soup kitchen at the brink of eviction. After all, Holland had been instrumental in putting a spotlight on the plight of Trenton's needy by, among other things, establishing a task force on homelessness and reaching out to those associated with TASK in making up the panel's membership. But with complaints piling up on his desk at City Hall, and the future of his core downtown redevelopment project, the Commons, hanging in the balance, the mayor concluded there was little choice in the matter: the soup kitchen had to go. "It's a question of trying to respond to two needs that are really incompatible," he told reporters. News of his position drew the immediate ire of TASK's more outspoken adherents, however, and harsh words were exchanged. The soup kitchen's chair, Terese Vogel Nelson (now married to one of the organization's founders, Rev. John Nelson), zapped Holland for seeking "to relocate the city's homeless and hungry to an area where no one can see them." The mayor, in turn, termed such remarks "irresponsible" and "uncalled-for." Betty Holland distinctly remembers the countervailing pressures that came to bear on her husband. "It was a very difficult time for him," she says. "I know he was upset by it, but he tried to do what was right by both groups."

Amid the back-and-forth, of course, the immediate question that loomed for everyone was "what now?" And if the city's leadership could be faulted for anything, it was in being utterly unprepared to provide a reasonable answer. While TASK received a bit of a reprieve when United Methodist's trustees extended the eviction deadline for one month, there was no real prospect of a home thereafter. No other churches were willing or able to play host, and the city's Rescue Mission, assumed by many (including the mayor) to be a natural candidate because of its shelter facilities, could accommodate no more than 60 people at a sitting and was determined to be too small. The most promising alternative emerged in the form of a Salvation Army center on the eastern end of State Street away from downtown, but it quickly became apparent that renovations were necessary to bring the place up to code for serving food to large numbers. Bottom line: TASK would either have to suspend operations or wind up out in the early spring cold. And although some sort of temporary shutdown made sense from a number of standpoints, not the least of which was that it would allow everyone to take a deep breath and regroup, anyone who might have been counting on that was to be sorely mistaken.

On April 1, 1986, in what, for the city at least, turned out to be an apt edition of April Fool's Day, the soup kitchen re-opened for business—in an unpaved parking lot adjacent to St. Michael's Episcopal Church on Perry Street. As volunteers heated soup and coffee on a stove in the church's tiny kitchen and handed out juice and brown-bag lunches from the back of a car—a sandwich, cookies, a piece of fruit—some 75 people milled about eating while standing for lack of tables and chairs. The media had a field day. One visitor told *The Times* "he felt like an animal in a zoo as he ate what would be his only meal of the day in a dirt lot." Another said, "'I've got to bite my sandwich between the dust and there's not even a place to wash your hands when you're done eating. It shows people think we're scum.'" One soup kitchen official speculated the open-air meal service would probably continue for weeks, adding, "'But where we'll be in six months to a year from now is anybody's guess.'"

Bleak as the situation seemed, it bore a silver lining. To be sure, this was a crisis for the hungry and homeless, but for those who made a living at city politics, it was a public relations nightmare of lapel-grabbing proportions—an embarrassment compounded by the fact that just a few blocks away from this heavily publicized feed lot, surplus tax revenues were pouring into the State of New Jersey's budget coffers. The debacle shamed at least some of those in power to take a closer look at their priorities. It certainly got Holland's attention. According to then-TASK Chair Cynthia Krommes, the mayor geared up the machinery of his office and directed his staff to assist in a move to the Salvation Army building, cutting red tape to expedite the permit process "even though their kitchen technically wasn't up to code." She also recalls him pledging city funds to assist with upgrading the facility and then participating directly in the subsequent, long-term search for a larger venue dedicated solely to TASK. "It was just a mess for him politically, being portrayed as some kind of Simon Legree figure, kicking the poor in the teeth and that sort of thing," says Krommes, among those who thought Holland, for the most part, was on the receiving end of a bum rap for the whole affair. "I think he stepped up for us, he really did. I can remember him later on picking me up in his car, and driving around looking for buildings that might be suitable for us to rehabilitate."

Meanwhile, that summer, as TASK settled in with the Salvation Army at 575 East State Street, discussion about the future took on new urgency. The lease was only good for six months—as it turned out, just the start of its temporary digs at that location. Going forward, the soup kitchen would have to rely on the Salvation Army's generosity for some five years. On top of that, the preceding weeks of nomadic uncertainty had shaken loose some fundamental questions the organizers had never fully confronted but which now begged resolution. What exactly was the soup kitchen's mission? Was it merely a place to hand out food? Where did it fit in the broader spectrum of helping the poor? How big should it be? How long could a nonprofit do this? Should it be permanent? Have its own facility? Was there a choice? To some, it was a no-brainer: five years of service and growth—and no end in sight to the need. But others harbored serious reservations and questioned the ultimate wisdom of putting down roots.

Isles Inc.'s Marty Johnson, who became involved in a committee to study the relocation matter, recalls many hours spent wrestling with these and other thorny matters. "There was a division among those who cared deeply about this," he says, "and it really cut along the lines of those who felt we should do everything we could to make hunger go away and not treat it symptomatically and those who were saying, 'Come on, this problem is here now, it's in front of us, we can't treat people like this by moving around all the time.'" Johnson counted himself among the skeptics. He feared the enterprise was shaping up as a mere Band-Aid in the face of deeper problems underlying poverty. For his part, Art Stanley recalls a point where it became obvious to most that the organization had to move beyond the food component and find a place where it could offer a wider array of services or risk defining itself as little more than a hunger warehouse. "We'd been at this long enough by then to realize there needed to be more to this than just soup and sandwiches," Stanley says. "We realized there were a lot of other needs and felt there was an opportunity to address the broader social-service aspect."

But if that were to be the course TASK would follow—to establish itself as a fixed provider of multiple services—it would require, at minimum, unprecedented fund-raising and a real-estate commitment of the sort that so far had eluded the organization. As the group debated and strategized its way to a rough consensus, Johnson recalls something resembling a moment of clarity. It came one evening when he and some of the others had gathered at a local diner. "We were having a fairly robust discussion, sometimes a bit heated, and a man nearby who had been overhearing all of it wrote an I.O.U. to us on a napkin for a couple hundred bucks. I'll never forget it. He'd been moved by the discussion and wanted to be part of the solution. And we thought that was a bit of an omen, a good sign that maybe there was adequate support out there for both things—for creating a facility now while keeping an open mind about whether this was a good thing we were investing in or a necessary evil, about whether it could let those in leadership in both the public and private sectors off the hook in dealing with the systemic nature of hunger."

As subsequent events made plain, sometimes painfully so, public support for a permanent Trenton-based soup kitchen cut different ways and depended largely on where you lived.

Money, of course, or rather the lack thereof, presented constant headaches, and the looming need to finance the construction of a new home was tantamount to a migraine. At the time, TASK's savings only amounted to about $40,000, which meant it had no choice but to undertake a titanic fund-raising effort. What the organization lacked in physical roots, though, it made up for in the energy of its boosters and in the scope of its reputation, which was already was solidly grounded. As a result, people in droves dug deep to help meet the substantial target estimate of some $600,000 for a well-equipped structure of suitable size. According to Irwin Stoolmacher, a local consultant who implemented and oversaw the campaign—and stuck through subsequent years to become TASK's long-term fund-raising consultant—scores of area companies and more than a dozen foundations joined with churches, labor unions and other organizations to support the project. As the months wore on, the project received generous set-piece grants, including a $50,000 check from United Parcel Service, along with more than 2,500 individual donations. At one point, *The Times* put the full force of its Trenton area Christmas appeal at TASK's disposal, pulling in more than $100,000—the first time the newspaper had ever designated a single organization as the sole recipient of proceeds from its annual charitable drive.

Money aside, however, the biggest obstacle facing TASK in its search for a home—as per an abundance of recent experience—was, collectively, "the neighbors." It seemed that no matter where the organization looked for a lot to develop or a building to renovate, community opposition followed. Succinctly put, "'Not-in-my-backyard' was very strong," says Virginia Link, who served for many years as TASK's board secretary.

Part of the dilemma was that the search, almost by default, focused exclusively on one area—the city's North Ward, a logical choice given its concentrated poverty, block upon block of dilapidated housing and commercial decay stretching from Perry Street to the vicinity of the Battle Monument and beyond. And by the fall of 1986, a prime candidate turned up there—a small abandoned department store along Pennington Avenue on property owned by the Roman Catholic Church. Though damaged by fire, the structure was sound, and a deal was struck with the Diocese of Trenton to convey the property to TASK, secured by a $2,500 down payment. But as word of the arrangement spread, nearby residents gave it a hearty thumbs-down, and they found a powerful advocate in the person of the late Albert "Bo" Robinson, their outspoken representative on City Council. Robinson knew full well the project would not be viable without the requisite sign-off by municipal planning and construction officials, and he was determined to keep the proper paperwork from seeing the light of day. Though this smacked of selfish NIMBYism at its worst, Robinson's stance was not entirely unreasonable; after all, he did have a responsibility to his constituents.

Besides, as he saw it, the North Ward, already heavily burdened by the trappings of poverty, now was being asked to shoulder even more. Ironically, TASK itself may have been one of the opposition's most assiduous, albeit unwitting, enablers by virtue of the fact that it had obviously failed to take adequate advance steps to soften the beachhead, to allay rumor and fear among people naturally suspicious about what they took to be unwarranted intrusion by outsiders. Indeed, the very complexion of the organization's governing board didn't help, says Steve Leder, an activist attorney who became the TASK's board chair in the latter stages of this difficult period. "It was made up primarily of white suburbanites, and there was not an aggressive outreach effort for minorities. To put it bluntly, there was this feeling that the soup kitchen was a bunch of blue-haired ladies from Princeton."

With the Pennington Avenue site effectively scotched, TASK was left with little choice but to negotiate a lease extension with the Salvation Army heading into 1987. Then, in something of a flash from the past, the organization abruptly received the offer of another North Ward lot a few blocks away along Allen Street owned by Mt. Zion A.M.E. Church—the very place that had got tangled in the city's permit bureaucracy six years earlier when it sought to be the soup kitchen's first host. Having since come into possession of several small parcels of land, Mt. Zion invited TASK to work out a plan under which one of the properties would be developed under a lease arrangement for joint use by both organizations. A building committee was established under the leadership of TASK volunteer Edward Gilman, and design work got under way—boosted by the enthusiastic endorsement of Mayor Holland, who declared the site "a dream location."

As it turned out, local planners and developers felt the same way—but for far different reasons. Almost simultaneously, they approached the city with blueprints for new and rehabilitated housing in the area, upwards of 200 units in all, a promising stride toward comprehensive redevelopment—and the economic equivalent of an offer municipal officials simply could not refuse. And there was a catch: the deal would be off the table if a soup kitchen or anything like it were allowed to take up residence around the corner. Councilman Robinson and his minions weighed in again with popular opposition as well, but they needn't have bothered. The housing initiative alone was sufficient to block TASK and keep it adrift. What ensued was an unseemly public spectacle that featured, on one hand, the city's chief executive eating his own words and, on the other, soup kitchen proponents blasting his administration for an about-face. Art Stanley and a colleague, Dr. David Fluck, went so far as to resign in protest from the city's hunger and homelessness task force. "He's backing developers over hungry people," Fluck, a prominent retired physician and chairman of the hunger panel, bluntly told reporters. Stanley recognized Holland was caught in an untenable political bind but recalls a compelling sense that something had to give—and it wasn't going to come from TASK's side of the ledger. "We knew he would support us when he could," Stanley says, "but we just felt this was terribly inconsistent on his part, and we felt the need to make a point. The basic problem was that the soup kitchen was a thorn in everybody's side, and nobody wanted to deal with the issue. Many just wished it would go away." The mayor took a heavy hit on the editorial pages, too, especially after he appeared to scold the soup kitchen's leadership for taking a hard-line posture on relocation. *The Times* reminded the mayor that TASK was a source of significant service to the poor at no cost to taxpayers, lecturing him to stifle his criticism and, instead, award the organization "proclamations, recognition days and medals" for its good works.

Months later came a bittersweet denouement.

On a cold day in early December 1987, Holland and TASK's leaders reconciled their differences with a handshake and a deal to end the organization's orphan status once and for all. The city agreed to donate a vacant plot of municipal land on Escher Street and, later on, at the mayor's behest, followed up with an offer to float $300,000 in municipal bonds to help finance construction of a new building. Faded newspaper photographs memorializing the land-transfer formalities show Gilman, Stanley and Crystal Smith, TASK's director at the time, peering over Holland's shoulder as if to make sure he is actually signing the requisite paperwork. As captured in the picture, their faint smiles also suggested something else: Escher Street clearly was nobody's first choice. Located deep in the North Ward on the far side of busy Route 1 a quarter-mile or so east of the recently disputed properties, this scruffy, out-of-the-way little lane didn't present the best neighborhood face in the world; in fact, the surroundings didn't amount to much of a neighborhood at all, more along the lines of a cluttered storage zone reserved for pieces of governmental infrastructure that have to be put some place—the police headquarters, maintenance facilities, an animal shelter and the like.

But what *was* the choice?

"We said, 'Hey, you're putting us out there with the dog pound and the police station and such,'" Stanley says. "But after a lot of discussion, we concluded it was a real opportunity." Vividly recollecting the mixed emotions swirling at the time, Steve Leder perhaps puts it best. "There's no question some people felt the site was insulting," he says, "But by and large, most of us on the board felt we were providing a valuable service and that the only way we were going to be able to continue doing that was if this place had a permanent home. And if people could come to it, well, that was the main thing." At least the price was right: one dollar a year for a city lease guaranteed for four decades.

Some three years after that lease was signed and the multiple challenges of site-search, design, fund-raising and construction were finally behind it, TASK dedicated its new home on July 1, 1991—a spacious 5,900-square-foot air-conditioned structure named in honor of Art Stanley and Ed Gilman. Gilman, a reserved, unassuming transportation engineer, shepherded the effort and is widely credited with providing the leadership required—"the quiet strength," in the words of one participant—to bring it all together based on plans drawn up free of charge by George Pearson, a local architect.

"It is our fervent hope that our patrons will have a choice when they come here," Leder, the organization's board chair at the time, told an audience of several hundred volunteers and supporters, politicians and public officials who gathered for the dedication ceremony. "If only a meal is desired, it will be cheerfully given. If additional services like health screening, job assessment and training, adult literacy, counseling or legal services are requested they will be made available. Many social service agencies have already agreed to use the soup kitchen as an outpost to provide a form of one-stop social service shopping.

"This building is meant to be a place for the community," he said, "a place of fellowship, learning and congeniality. Through your support, we are reminded that we are all our brothers' keepers."

·   ·   ·

Years later, during the fall of 2005, TASK marked a dubious milestone inside the Gilman-Stanley building, something many of the early volunteers would have found almost inconceivable (as did many of their 21st Century counterparts): the day the total number of meals served over the course of the organization's history topped two million. This benchmark gave pause not only to those concerned about the present and future of hunger and poverty, and about the role of the soup kitchen in it all, but it also served as a reminder of the past and of how the actions of a few can grow and develop and be nurtured into a response to the needs of many. And it raised an intriguing question: what became of that small circle of men and women who were among those present at the creation of this enterprise?

Art Holland succumbed to cancer in the fall of 1989 and never saw the lot he urged the city to donate come to fruition as the liveliest spot on Escher Street. But he did live long enough to enjoy the fruits of reconciliation with his occasional TASK adversaries, some of whom touched him deeply, Betty Holland says, with unsolicited visits to his hospital bedside. The organization also asked him to join its governing board, and, in a letter to his widow on November 10, 1989, then-TASK Chair Ed Gilman wrote, "Your husband was a friend to the soup kitchen and to those of us who went to see him on its behalf. We were honored to have him accept a place on our Board of Trustees. We shall certainly miss him."

John Weatherly left Trenton in the fall of 1987 at the height of TASK's real-estate search and followed an unusual path. He spent two years in missionary work in Brazil, then settled in Wilmington, N.C., where, he says, lessons learned in the struggle to get the soup kitchen situated served him well in overcoming local siting and zoning issues in the construction of a new church. He moved to Connecticut, then to Virginia as rector of St. Mark's Episcopal Church in Alexandria. Meanwhile, having enlisted in the Army National Guard—and following roughly in the footsteps of his father, a Navy Chaplain—Weatherly spent eight months deployed to Bosnia in 2001–02. In October 2005, he was called up again and dispatched to Iraq. "It's a rewarding ministry," he observed by e-mail in the fall of 2006. "But, lately, too heavy on the hospital visits."

Over the years, Weatherly was involved in three other soup kitchens around the U.S. He says that despite the ups and downs experienced by TASK, "I have never found the broad-based support among churches, politicians, volunteers and community leaders as I did in Trenton. There was a real willingness to provide for people in trouble, to make that one day a bit better, that sense of authentic compassion. I remember folks with very limited means continually stretching out to help someone in greater need—taking people home, giving them clothes, a job, or just sitting down and spending some time talking. No other place was as successful in getting people involved in community."

Weatherly's close friend, Marty Johnson, went on to establish Isles Inc. as one of the region's most effective nonprofit weapons against concentrated poverty. The organization's track record includes multiple successful programs in job training and placement, financial self-reliance, nutrition and environmental and community health. Recognized particularly for its housing initiatives, Isles has served as a catalyst in the transformation of blighted neighborhoods, notably Trenton's scarred Battle Monument area—the same dilapidated pocket of the city that had been targeted for redevelopment during the late 80s in a plan that forced TASK to look elsewhere for a permanent site. Resurrection of that project by Isles and the city more than a decade later resulted in a tidy new residential enclave of 84 brick-fronted town homes.

Despite such progress—or indeed, perhaps because of the very incremental nature of it—Johnson remains deeply skeptical about the future absent evidence of greater commitment by the public sector to a sustained assault on issues that create the need for job training, affordable housing and soup kitchens in the first place. "We've had this proliferation of nonprofit organizations around the country that are providing services to those who have fallen through the cracks," he says. "But how do we address the systemic nature of the problem? I think we've lost the edge on that type of substantive discussion." Once doubtful that TASK would become little more than an emblem of the symptomatic approach to dealing with poverty, Johnson has been impressed by its programmatic breadth. "It's a lot better than most soup kitchens around the country in trying to understand that hunger is just the beginning of a journey that has to be addressed on the way to self-reliance," he says. "But it's a very difficult job to be able to think about all of those other issues while trying to take care of so many people who are hungry."

Beverly Mills earned degrees in public administration and fine arts and spent the 90s as chef/owner at a restaurant called Flavors in her hometown of Pennington. "Once again I was feeding people," laughs TASK's second director, "but in a different way." Several years after exiting that business, she joined the public sector as deputy director of Mercer County's Workforce Investment Board, which, among other things, oversees the "One Stop" network of employment and job counseling centers. Mills says what has stuck with her about the soup kitchen experience after all these years is a sense of sadness tempered by human warmth. "I used to look at the people who went there and wonder how they got to that place, what happened in their lives that brought them there," she says. "What I discovered was that it's easier than most people can imagine to fall down. It can happen to anyone." At the same time, "these people, the patrons, they really made a whole family out of that place. They got to know each other and it was like one big extended family."

John and Terese Nelson wound up on Cape Cod where, he says, "what was supposed to be retirement" became a new "part-time" career in real estate construction in and around Provincetown. Terese connected with the community's public education system and was elected chair of the local school committee (the Yankee version of a school board). Between pouring over blueprints and building plans, John writes contemporary folk music and has actually recorded several CDs of original material in Nashville. From time to time, when his thoughts turn to Trenton and to TASK, what often comes to mind is a vivid recollection of the frenzied beginning, particularly images of Alice Parker pulling the soup kitchen together almost single-handedly on a daily basis. "I can tell you this," Nelson says, "the force of her personality and her no-nonsense aggressiveness is largely responsible for getting the original creaky ship out on the water and making it float."

Indeed, Parker has gone on to make many things "float." The Lifeline Shelter she established after leaving TASK in the mid-80s still provides a small but vital refuge for homeless women and children in Trenton. Working from a comfortable renovated house at the corner of Tyler Street and South Clinton Avenue, she also operates an emergency food pantry and presides over a self-named foundation that offers college scholarships and seed money for a variety of other initiatives linked to education. Only recently, slowed somewhat by a stroke and by cataracts that rendered her legally blind, has Parker begun to contemplate retirement. She has also spent a good deal of time rethinking the ultimate utility of soup kitchens and food pantries, worrying particularly about their apparent permanence, fearing that what is a necessity for some has, for others, become a way of life. "I was never in favor of that," Parker says. "I've been on this journey for 30 years, and I have learned that people will take what you're going to give them. And if you continue to give, they will continue to take. We have to ask, what do we really want to do? You can't just give people food; that's just the start of it, not the end of it. They need more than that to stabilize them, to get them to a point where they can say, 'I can do better than this.'"

And Art Stanley—the man behind the idea? He and Barbara finally did land in a country place, retiring to a small community near the Blue Ridge Mountains of Virginia. Looking back, Stanley can appreciate some of the ambivalence surrounding both TASK and the durability of the need it continues to serve. Indeed, having never really thought about the organization he helped to found so many years ago beyond the context of pure temporariness, his own emotions on the subject are quite mixed. "It's staggering to think about," he says. "On one hand, you have to be greatly impressed by the number of people who became involved and stayed involved and are continuing to be involved in reaching out to fill basic needs of food and shelter and education. That's a tremendous story. But there's that other side to it. We are the wealthiest nation that ever existed on the planet, and here we are still having to dish out food to the hungry. There's a disconnect, and a sadness, that people have to keep doing this after all these years.

"But at least we feel like we did what we could do, and we're grateful that others have come along to do the same."

3

Hunger, Inc.

Shortly before Christmas 2006, TASK broke ground on a major expansion to add several thousand square feet of sorely needed food-storage space, install upgraded kitchen equipment and provide more room for patrons, volunteers and staff. It had been a long time coming, this project—the culmination of nearly a half decade's worth of stop-and-start planning and design, fund-raising and bureaucratic arm-wrestling, meetings, bids, contract reviews, meetings, votes and more meetings. But here on this chill winter morning, with the big moment finally at hand, it was all smiles and pats on the back as members of the soup kitchen's board of trustees gathered with employees and supporters around a ceremonial shovel, the handle garnished with seasonal red ribbon, to pose for pictures. Afterwards, as we talked about what had been and what was to come, words like "milestone" hung in the air. "I can't believe it's finally happening," someone said. "It hasn't sunk in yet."

What had sunk in, though, at least to my way of thinking, was a disconcerting array of mixed emotions. Standing there with friends and colleagues, it felt good to be part of the effort, part of making the soup kitchen a bigger, better place so more people in need could be served. But it also felt awkward and uncomfortable—and not just because of the head-bobbing yellow hard-hat I had to wear for the photo op. For sure, this was a milestone; TASK had only undergone one previous expansion in its history, and that was small potatoes compared to this latest effort. So, yes, a milestone by any measure. But cause for celebration? How could it be? The very thought of having to do this—having to beg, borrow and wheedle more than a million dollars to make room for more service to still more hungry people—that thought was, well … repugnant, to be perfectly blunt, a striking little metaphor for the success of failure.

As the group broke up and I headed back to my car, another notion flooded my mind. It occurred to me that to an outsider or someone unfamiliar with the purpose of our little gathering, it might in passing have seemed the formal construction kick-off for just about anything. Groundbreakings, after all, are groundbreakings, and from a distance, this event, given its generic trappings, could just as well have been regarded as the launching of some sort of commercial venture, a new restaurant, say, or a bank branch, warehouse or office complex. I thought about how enterprises like that employ many people and serve many clients, customers and patrons. How, under the right economic conditions, optimal supply-and-demand and proper management, they grow and, from time to time, require investment and expansion. How, collectively, they make up entire industries. Mulling this over, it struck me that TASK is part of an industry, too—an industry that consumes its own vast share of capital, employs thousands of people and serves millions of consumers, a sprawling nationwide venture equipped with everything from warehouses and wholesale distributors to trucking fleets and retail outlets scattered coast to coast. Though it turns no profit, has no listing on the stock exchange and makes no headlines on the business pages, this industry's machinery, like that of any other going concern, is cranked up to meet the demands of a growing and demographically changing marketplace every day.

It is the hunger industry, and the nondescript building in front of which I now stood, waiting for the backhoes and bulldozers and workers to arrive to start putting on an addition, occupies just one tiny corner of it.

If you pursue this line of thinking to its logical conclusion, the plain fact is that the hunger industry is itself merely a piece of something larger. Just as banking and stock-brokering are but parts of the more expansive financial services sector, and in much the same way that res-taurants and supermarkets are diversified components of the global food industry, Hunger, Inc. is a subsidiary of a much broader enterprise, too—a multi-faceted, geographically boundless conglomerate that goes by many names but is known to most simply as poverty. And one of the main reasons business at the local soup kitchen is booming these days is that this, its parent company, has been on quite a tear over the course of the past decade, posting some spectacular numbers that, in another dimension, would constitute the sort of trend-line that routinely makes savvy Wall Streeters go weak at the knees over visions of year-end bonuses.

The difference, of course, and it is significant, is this: when it comes to the poverty conglomerate or any of its constituent parts, the bigger the numbers the worse it is for everyone.

But talk about a customer base. Nearly 40 million Americans today live in poverty—that is, in households with incomes below the official poverty line, pegged at not quite $20,000 a year. Between 2003 and 2006, that number rose by almost four million—an average annual growth rate in the neighborhood of 3 percent. But that doesn't tell the whole story. As with the sort of general data set forth at the outset of a typical corporate annual report, it's the "numbers behind the numbers," those at the back of the book or in the footnotes, that are really reveal-ing. Here's one: according to the U.S. Bureau of Labor Statistics, 43 percent of these households actually have incomes below *one-half* of the poverty line. Think about that. These are people who exist in a neth-erworld of privation so bad the bureaucrats call it "deep poverty," and their numbers are higher now than they have ever been since the gov-ernment began keeping a record of the phenomenon in the mid-1970s. Here's another: more than 12 million American children under 18 are growing up in poverty—nearly one-fifth of the nation's generation of the future. In New Jersey, children have become what has been described as "the fastest growing segment of the underclass." A survey released in 2007 by the advocacy group, the Association for Children of New Jersey, showed that there were 35 percent more children aged five and younger living in poverty than four years earlier. At what cost? Aside from the obvious and incalculable human suffering, child poverty robs the U.S. economy to the tune of at least $500 million a year because as these disadvantaged youngsters age, they are less productive, have lower earning power, commit more crime and generate more health-related costs than the population at large, according to an exhaustive study commissioned by the Washington-based Center for American Progress and released in early 2007.

And just like any other market-driven economic venture, poverty is stronger in some places than others—even under circumstances where that might seem a paradox. Take New Jersey, for example. Measured strictly by per capita income, TASK's home is one of the nation's wealthiest states, a place where logic might dictate a minor opportunity for poverty. But partnered with that platinum marker of wealth is the fact that New Jersey is also one of the most expensive states in which to try to make a living. Housing, food, transportation, child care, health care, insurance—you name it, it costs more in the Garden State than in most of the rest of the country. That means the basic poverty statistics, which show 740,000 residents eking out a living below the official income threshold (8.5 percent of the population), simply don't get close to delineating the actual extent of poverty across the state. Indeed, numerous studies have shown that given New Jersey's high cost of living, the poverty threshold within its borders should more fairly be pegged at a household income of at least $40,000—twice the official level set by the federal government. By that yardstick, the number of New Jerseyans in poverty more than doubles to 1.8 million men, women and children—*fully 20 percent of the state's entire population.* And if data gathered and analyzed by one organization, the Washington, D.C-based Economic Policy Institute, is anywhere near accurate, even that number is substantially understated. EPI has estimated that in order to maintain a modest standard of living, a two-parent, two-child household actually requires annual income of between $45,000 and $53,000.

Among the poverty conglomerate's various subsidiary industries, affordable housing—or, rather, *un*affordable housing—has been a particularly potent performer. Here's why: it is widely accepted by experts in this field that no more than 30 percent of a household's monthly income should be spent putting a roof over your head. Otherwise, you and your family risk not having enough money left to cover food, transportation, insurance and other essentials, let alone the occasional minor extravagance. To figure out what that means in real dollars, the non-profit Housing and Community Development Network of New Jersey did the math and found that better than half the state's more than one million tenants in 2006 could not afford the average monthly rent for a two-bedroom apartment. To do so, the organization estimated, would have required an income of more than $44,000 a year. That's equal to a job paying $21 and change per hour, before taxes. At the minimum wage, then $7.15 an hour, forget it. Someone would have had to endure a whopping 119-hour work week—the equivalent of almost three full-time jobs—to reach the realm of affordability. Who is priced out? Social workers (average salary: $40,190); librarians (average salary: $28,430); hair stylists (average salary: $25,510), to name just a few examples. In other words, those whose incomes used to put them in the middle class, or at least in close proximity to it, but who are now falling into an oxymoronic category called "the working poor." The practical effect of the cost-crunch they face, of course, is that more and more people, singles and families alike, are squeezing into one-bedroom and studio apartments, moving in with relatives or finding other living arrangements. And with increasing frequency, in order to make ends meet, they are having to choose between paying the rent, turning down the heat, foregoing necessary medical care or even going without a meal several times a week or more. Which, of course, is where the hunger industry comes into play.

According to America's Second Harvest (A2H), the largest food-bank network in the country, the number of households at risk of hunger has nearly doubled over the last 20 years, and demand for emergency food is up nearly 10 percent over the past decade. This despite explosive growth in the nation's overall economy, billions spent by the government on food stamps and other poverty relief programs and the presumed effect of so-called welfare-to-work "reforms" in the nation's public assistance apparatus. In 1980, there were only about two dozen food banks scattered around the U.S.; today, their number tops 200. They supply some 30,000 food pantries, 5,600 soup kitchens and more than 4,000 emergency shelters—operated mostly by the nonprofit sector. Demand is up appreciably in every category. In all, more than 25 million people, including nine million children and three million senior citizens, now rely temporarily or chronically on these types of charitable facilities for food. More than one-third of the time, A2H reports, someone in these needy households is employed. The system of dispensing emergency food has become so entrenched, in fact, that it has spawned an entire profession of career-oriented workers—"food bankers," they are called—who started as volunteers and now hold full-time salaried positions complete with health benefits and pension plans. One disturbing indicator of just exactly how this industry has matured is that, in many instances, those pension plans are now being activated at an increasing rate as more and more leaders of food banks, soup kitchens and other nonprofit agencies enter their retirement years. Indeed, studies suggest that close to three-quarters of present nonprofit agency directors will retire, die or otherwise disappear from the scene within the next five years. Who will take their place?

Several dramatic changes in the broader socio-economic and demographic scheme of things provide a backdrop for the trends underlying these developments in the poverty conglomerate.

The most prominent, of course, is widening income disparity in the U.S. The income gaps that exist today between the wealthiest Americans and the poorest—and between the wealthiest and the middle class—are greater than they have been in decades. The wealthiest Americans, the top 1 percent, now receive more than 20 percent of the nation's income—their largest share since the years immediately preceding the Great Depression. Those beneath that level of wealth, meanwhile, have seen their incomes stagnate. Look at any study, crunch the numbers any way you see fit, but the reality is undeniable: trite and clichéd though it may sound, the rich *are* getting richer, and the poor *are* getting poorer, and most of the people in between are being pulled toward the lower end of the equation.

Second, poverty has begun recruiting heavily in the suburbs. A 2005 Brookings Institution study of the hundred largest metropolitan areas in the U.S. found that for the first time, the suburban poor outnumbered their inner-city counterparts. Even though the actual rate of poverty remained higher in urban areas, the Brookings study revealed that because of shifts in population growth, suburban communities now were home to 12.2 million poor people compared to 11 million in the contiguous cities—clearly a sign of corrosion in the outer ring of wealth. "Economies are regional now," Alan Berube, the report's co-author, told The Associated Press. "Looking back at the 1970s, you would have seen cities suffering and suburbs staying the same. But the story is different today.... Where you see increases in city poverty, in almost every metropolitan area, you also see increases in suburban poverty." Data gathered by America's Second Harvest during 2005 and 2006 appear to bear this out. The organization reports that nearly 50 percent of the recipients of emergency food from pantries around the country now live in rural and suburban communities.

Meanwhile, volunteers and workers on the front lines of the poverty/hunger complex—those on the serving side of the counter at the retail level, so to speak—have witnessed a pronounced and alarming transformation in the very shape and face of the need walking through their front doors every day. Besides larger numbers and the rise of the working poor, those desperate for help these days often carry with them a complex tangle of mental and physical baggage that a simple meal and a warm cot don't come close to addressing. Mary Gay Abbot-Young, chief executive officer of the Rescue Mission of Trenton—operator of one of New Jersey's leading homeless shelters and a host of related service programs—has nearly 30 years' experience in these trenches, and she has seen it all. "When I first came here," she says, "the population was primarily World War II veterans, guys of that age who had, in effect, drunk themselves down to skid row. Most of them had families, their education was at least average and they usually had some kind of skill—carpenters, electricians, that sort of thing. Now, they're younger, more aggressive, with less education and more mental health issues. They don't have the job skills or the work ethic we'd seen. They didn't drink themselves into poverty. They were born there." One especially nasty and protracted wrinkle: what to do about overwhelming numbers of former prison inmates, many of them repeat drug offenders, who are now being released as their terms expire only to find the community ill-equipped to help them re-enter society. "Everybody says, 'Let's have a program for the ex-offender.' Well, the ex-offender's got fifty zillion problems that come with him," says Abbot-Young. "It isn't just the fact that he's an ex-offender, or that he's got a drug problem, or that he has limited education, or mental issues, or that his family has disintegrated and on and on. You put all of those things together, and they start running around each other."

Out in the suburbs, in Lawrenceville, a community located between Trenton and the affluent confines of Princeton, Connie Mercer runs an operation called HomeFront, whose comprehensive services include a food pantry, counseling and the provision of shelter for the homeless. "This used to be a straight-forward problem everyone could understand," Mercer says, "but now it's far more complicated. What we've got now are more and more folks with severe mental illness or with drug problems." Particularly vexing, she says, is the challenge presented by so many impoverished young women who are turning up for help. "Many of the women we're dealing with now were raised by moms who were strung out on drugs. Some were drug babies, crack babies, and some of them lived through such horrors because their moms were not able to parent at all. So they don't know how to cook a meal. They don't know how to organize a day. They don't know any of the basic life skills because there was no order in their lives."

Though advocates are encouraged by the level of volunteer support they see in the wider community and by clear signs that some politicians are willing to put their money where their mouths are—Gov. Jon Corzine, for one, earmarked $4 million in his first state budget to fight hunger, a pittance against overall state spending but nonetheless a first for New Jersey—those on the front lines are not exactly sanguine about the future. During the relatively mild early-winter months of 2006–07, the Rescue Mission had to scramble to keep up with the demand for its services. "The number of people coming here needing help is up, and the level of help they need is so much greater," say Abbot-Young. "We've got a lot going for us here, but we're still losing the battle."

•   •   •

Okay, time for a field trip. Drive north out of Trenton on the Turnpike for about 50 miles to Exit 14, then head west on Route 22, careful not to take a wrong turn amid the vehicular chaos that surrounds Newark Liberty International Airport. In a few minutes, the sooty concrete sprawl gives way on your left to an incongruous park-like setting of wooded greenswards—the fairways of Weequaic Golf Course, demarking the city limits of Newark. Another half-mile or so and you're in Hillside, a gritty industrial burg bisected by rail lines and roads worn by heavy diesel traffic. At the flashing red light, hang a right onto Broad Street, then a sharp left onto Evans Terminal Road, winding down a gently sloping hill past a machine-parts factory, a construction supply depot and a scattering of other low-slung buildings, all the way to the bottom until you can go no farther. There, looming two stories high and running like a fortress wall for what seems like 500 yards in both directions, the near-end of it thrown wide open to truck bays and loading docks, sits one very large and, judging by the number of vehicles parked outside, one very busy manufacturing plant and/or warehouse. Indeed, up until the early 90s, Kraft Foods turned out tons upon tons of its signature Parkay margarine here. And food is still the *raison d'etre* of this cavernous structure, but for a far different purpose. These days it's a flagship facility in the ever-expanding portfolio of Hunger, Inc.—the Community FoodBank of New Jersey.

This place is so big—280,000-odd square feet, the equivalent of a half-dozen regulation soccer fields stitched together—that to tour it in less than an hour without getting lost, I'd advise you to climb aboard one of several battery-powered golf carts donated over the years to afford the staff efficient mobility. You'll pass aisle after aisle of towering storage racks packed to the rafters with pallets containing huge shrink-wrapped blocks of canned meat, vegetables and tuna fish, fruit juice, pasta and myriad other foodstuffs. Forklifts prowl the space, hauling their loads to and from a small fleet of trucks as a booming loudspeaker bellows announcements and workers and volunteers sort through bags and boxes. Three large refrigerated coolers provide temporary storage for fresh produce, eggs and milk while a pair of giant freezers—including a recent $350,000 addition that seems the size of a small airplane hanger—hold bulk supplies of poultry and meat. More than 23 million pounds of food pass through this place every year on the way to serve an estimated 500,000 people in most of New Jersey's 21 counties. Were this part of a private business, its annual revenues, based upon the total value of product moved, would top $60 million.

"People hear the term food bank and think we're some place that's got a room with a few shelves and some canned goods we hand out," says Kathleen DiChiara, the organization's founder, chief executive officer and top tour guide. "We *are* part of an industry, and so we have to look at the standards and processes that go with being a business. Basically, what we've done here I think is make the leap from being do-gooders to doing good, and the bridge between those two is operating with sound business principles."

Tall and soft-spoken, DiChiara greets visitors with a quick smile, a handshake and a few murmurs of small talk, but there is about her the slightly impatient air of a person with many things on her mind and little time to waste. First impressions tell you this is someone who landed in the nonprofit sector after a successful career in the corporate world, who traded pantsuits for work pants and made a seamless transition with all the acquired diplomatic and management skills necessary to pull it together. Work pants, yes. But the rest of it? Couldn't be further from the truth. In fact, DiChiara herself still marvels at the wholly unexpected and uninvited chain of circumstances that propelled her to become the architect of this remarkable enterprise. "This all started out of the backseat of my station wagon," she says matter-of-factly. "And if someone at the time had asked me how would you like to give 30 years of your life to a cause, I would have said absolutely not. I was a suburban housewife with two small children.

"But, one day at a time, it did happen."

An elementary school teacher by training and homemaker by vocation, DiChiara, by her own admission, wasn't exactly preoccupied back in 1975 with the difference between clothes lines and bottom lines, and she certainly wasn't spending a good deal of her time dwelling on the nature and extent of hunger and poverty. But then one Sunday morning, she was sitting in church with her family when the priest, delivering a sermon about famine in Africa, asked parishioners to give up meat twice a week as a way of empathizing with those in need. For her part, DiChiara thought it might make more sense if people donated money saved by cutting back on meat to the poor closer to home. So she took it upon herself to explore the level of need in and around her hometown of Summit and quickly found plenty of it, particularly among the elderly. She started collecting canned goods and launched a program called "Loaves and Fishes," using her garage for storage and her own family car to make an ever-widening circle of deliveries. One regular stop on the route was the home of old woman who lived alone and whose circumstances so touched DiChiara that she felt compelled to set the experience down in words, a story, she says, that inspires her efforts to this day:

> *Mathilde was one of the very first people I brought food to when I was first starting out. She was 93, owned her own home, and her only source of income was a small Social Security check that oftentimes did not make it through the month. She was a woman who had worked hard all her life, and she had a great deal of pride. It took a number of visits—and time for a friendship to develop—before I could get her to accept a bag of groceries.*
>
> *She wanted so much to do something in return for the food. She loved to garden but had become too frail to dig.... For three summers, my children and I dug up her garden plot and helped as she planted a dozen tomato plants, carrots, cabbage and squash.*

All summer, she cared for the plants, watering them, weeding them, and finally harvesting the ripened vegetables. With great pride she would hand me a bag of vegetables from her garden so I might share them with others. The summer that she died, I would often find her sitting on the ground in the garden, with a rope that led back to the porch tied around her waist. This way, if she fainted or was too weak to walk (she was dying of cancer), she could pull herself back to the porch using the rope.

Before she died, she gave me a little metal Sucrets box filled with pennies. She said, "Use this for the children—it's so hard to be hungry when you are little."

DiChiara's efforts soon outgrew her home, and she organized a string of pantries, which, in turn, led to the establishment of an emergency food program covering a four-county area of northern New Jersey under the auspices of the Catholic Archdiocese of Newark. By the early 80s, it was readily apparent that, burgeoning though her own local hunger-service operation had become, it was really just one small part of a much larger picture. She learned that a group of like-minded people in Phoenix, Arizona, had begun to pool efforts around a broad-based regional assault on hunger, directly soliciting core elements of the food industry—manufacturers, wholesale distributors and retail supermarket chains—for leftovers, damaged but otherwise edible canned goods and other commodities. The strategy involved cut-rate food purchases or outright donations in bulk, which would be stored centrally, divided into manageable lots and delivered to soup kitchens, homeless shelters and emergency pantries. In 1982 (the same year, by happenstance, that TASK was founded), she and her small team of organizers determined that this broader network approach offered a more flexible, efficient and effective future for their efforts, so they parted ways with the Catholic Church and joined forces with what was to become the nationwide hunger-battling system known as America's Second Harvest.

Today, with an annual budget of nearly $7 million, 102 full-time employees and a food-handling volume roughly four times that of the average-sized food bank, this busy little corner of industrial Hillside—along with a 28,000-square-foot branch facility in South Jersey's

Egg Harbor Township—boasts the second largest food bank operation in the country outside of the A2H headquarters facility, now based in Chicago. Since its inception, the Community FoodBank of New Jersey has distributed some 400 million pounds of food and groceries. Giant facilities like this serve as key transshipment points for New Jersey's share of some $140 million worth of surplus commodity foods—everything from canned and dried fruits to beans, butter and pasta—made available every year through the USDA and its Emergency Food Assistance Program. For its own part, the Community FoodBank of New Jersey's fleet of trucks, including a pair of custom-painted 53-foot tractor trailers, make deliveries every day to nearly 1,000 charitable organizations, and the goods keep moving thanks in large part to a veritable army of more than 21,000 volunteers.

But this is more than just a hunger warehouse. "Every time we've grown," DiChiara says, "I've tried to use it as an opportunity to provide jobs, particularly jobs for people who might be at a soup kitchen or a shelter or just out of prison. Sixty percent of my staff are ex-offenders or addicts in recovery." A while back, the organization installed a fully-equipped commercial kitchen to train people for employment in the restaurant and food-service industry. Recruited from social-service agencies, halfway houses and welfare-to-work programs, students who join the 14-week program learn the culinary arts, in part, by turning out a low-cost lunch for the staff several days a week. Upon graduation, they can look forward to a nearly 100 percent job-placement rate—even given some strict caveats set forth by the food bank's management: prospective jobs, for example, must pay at least $9 an hour and provide full benefits. Kitchen academy alumni have gone on to work in such places as New York City's Tavern on the Green.

The food-service training center plays a particularly critical role in fulfilling a multi-dimensional commitment the organization has made to disadvantaged children. Through a project dubbed the "Kids Café," the kitchen prepares dinner for delivery every weekday evening to after-school programs attended by hundreds of at-risk youngsters. In 2004, the food bank also started providing local schools with supplemental food for needy children to take home. Each is given a back-pack of the sort any youngster would tote back and forth to school, except that every Friday afternoon, these special back-packs are unobtrusively filled with food bank-supplied boxes of juice and milk, crackers, a couple of containers of apple sauce or diced peaches, a packet of Pop-Tarts and two canned meals—beef stew, spaghetti and the like. "These are kids who have been identified by teachers or school officials who are concerned that they may not be eating very much or very well over the weekend," DiChiara explains.

Aside from nutrition, the food bank offers children clothing—not just hand-me-downs, but brand new clothing in the form of three to five complete outfits per child a year—under an arrangement worked out with various manufacturers and retailers. And, in partnership with the School, Home and Office Products Association, the organization provides school supplies. One afternoon each semester, teachers from 160 inner-city schools in North Jersey can visit a large room tucked away in the warehouse that resembles a well-stocked stationery store and gather up books, paper, tape, pens, colored markers, arts and crafts materials, you name it, all free of charge. "Being a teacher myself by education, I know how difficult it is to assign homework to children who don't have paper or pencils," says DiChiara. She also appreciates the importance of maintaining accountability in the midst of charity and makes a point of noting that her organization checks to make sure the organization's largess actually reaches the hands of its intended recipients. The classrooms of teachers who participate in the supply giveaway, for example, receive regular visits from food-bank personnel. "We're proud of our reputation in that regard," she says. "It makes it easier to solicit the goods in the first place because we can show it's not going to a flea market or something like that."

When not traversing the vast food storage and transshipment area, greeting volunteers and cajoling workers, DiChiara can usually be found in a spacious second-floor nook that houses the food bank's business offices. On one side of the building here, a wall of windows opens onto a roof that's been converted into a sort of makeshift garden with benches. Staffers who take periodic respites for a stroll in the fresh air, though, have learned to stay alert or risk getting plunked. The first hole of the Weequaic links is just beyond the trees, and from spring through fall, over-shooting duffers regularly deposit golf balls onto the pathways between the planters. Some years ago, after accumulating a sizable quantity of errant Slazengers, Titleists and Top Flites, each one bearing a trademark tar-paper smudge, DiChiara hit upon the idea of using them as a fund-raising gimmick. Now, they are sought-after premium items at the organization's annual "Blue Jean Ball" held right downstairs in the warehouse.

Opposite the walk-out rooftop is a clutter-comfortable office suite full of tables and shelves piled with papers, folders and books, its walls covered in framed memorabilia—plaques, posters and photographs, including several featuring the smiling face of singer/songwriter Bruce Springsteen, a prominent supporter. This is where the key decisions are made, where food shipments are monitored and trends are tracked, where tallies are kept and bottlenecks resolved and where plans are hatched and nurtured to keep up with the growth of what DiChiara calls an ever-changing "forever project."

"It's getting bigger, and it's getting more complicated," she says, settling into a chair near her desk. "We're able to maximize people's donations in so many ways, and yet, in reality, it does cost money to run our freezers and our trucks, and it costs money to employ as many people as we employ." The form and shape of the physical resource-base is changing as well, and the food bank has undertaken a number of initiatives, including equipping its computer network with software upgrades, to reap efficiencies and keep up with it all. For example, "the food that was once available in multiple trailer loads is much more difficult to track down now," DiChiara says. "We're having to go farther for it and spend more money to get it." What's more, as a result of technical improvements in packaging and inventory control at the manufacturing end of the food industry, there has been a marked reduction in recent years in the available volume of "reclaimed" products—dented canned goods, mislabeled items, etc. These trends, which are national in scope, have forced the food bank to explore alternatives, including a more active solicitation of outlets at the retail level. The organization has also embarked upon an effort to launch a line of its own brand-name products for sale to the public ala actor Paul Newman's charitable business enterprise.

"It's all part of our mission in fighting hunger and poverty," DiChiara says. "For myself, I guess it's okay to know that in my lifetime I probably won't see the solution to it all. But that doesn't discourage me from working on it because I've seen inroads made. Even with these increases in demand, I've also seen more and more people get involved. There's a quotation I have on the wall someplace around here that says something to the effect, 'It's not going to be the experts who are going to solve this. It'll be when you and I decide we want to make it happen.'"

•   •   •

Once a week, a loaded tractor trailer pulls away from the Community FoodBank's loading dock and heads south toward Trenton. The destination: a nondescript commercial office park in suburban Ewing Township. There, in a low-slung, tan stucco building surrounded by insurance agencies, transport companies, sportswear distributors and storage outlets, sits a most unlikely addition to this little colony of entrepreneurship—the Mercer Street Friends (MSF) Food Bank. But don't be fooled by sedate appearances. Beyond the glass doors of this structure is a 10,000-square-foot warehouse that serves as a transshipment point for nearly two million pounds of food distributed every year to charities throughout Mercer County, home of New Jersey's capital. It is fully equipped with an expansive, tail-gate-level loading dock for truck deliveries and pick-ups, machinery for stacking and storing pallets, a walk-in refrigerator and freezer and a large area where volunteers stationed at tables have plenty of elbow room to sort, box and bag a wide selection of goods. In the peculiar corporate world that is Hunger, Inc., where the sprawling Community FoodBank of New Jersey is analogous to the manufacturing plant, Mercer Street Friends is the wholesaler—the "middle-man," so to speak—that deals directly with street-level retail charities like TASK.

"We provide food directly to the soup kitchen, to emergency shelters, to food pantries, day-care centers, after-school programs and others," says Phyllis Stoolmacher, director of the MSF food bank. "We either give it to them for free or at very low cost, and the number of places we serve has just escalated continuously. It just doesn't end in terms of the charities coming forward and saying we need to do something about hunger." Indeed, Mercer Street Friends moved its food distribution operation here in mid-2006 after years of struggling to function amid rising demand and dwindling space in the cramped confines of a former postal branch building along Trenton's Brunswick Avenue. "It got so that I was having to turn food away every week because we couldn't get it physically into the warehouse," Stoolmacher says. "The parking lot there was never built to handle 53-foot-long tractor trailers. It was maybe 55 feet, and they could barely turn around." The organization's new facility nearly tripled the available storage space, and, though the 10-year lease carries significant cost, "it's worth every penny because it allows us to increase not only the volume of the food but the kind of food we offer." Exhibit A: the spanking new walk-in (actually closer in size to a drive-in) refrigeration and freezer units that now enable the organization to receive, store and move a steady stream of prized perishables, everything from eggs and margarine to fresh meat, poultry, even frozen fish. Speaking of the latter, the MSF food operation hadn't occupied this new facility for more than six months when it became quite apparent that yet more freezer space was warranted. One afternoon, a truck pulled up to unload 150 cases of USDA surplus chicken—the same day the food bank was expecting a big load of frozen whiting. Something had to give. "We had to postpone the fish because it wouldn't fit," Stoolmacher says, "but we don't want to have to make decisions like that." The answer will be a new $50,000 freezer capable of holding up to 14 fully stacked pallets at a time, nearly double the existing freezer space. In front of the cooling units, rising at least 20 feet above the floor and running for maybe 20 yards along the middle of the warehouse are pallets of cereal—generic Cheerios, hundreds of boxes bound in large shrink-wrapped blocks that arrived by truck just the other day. "Back in our other place," says Stoolmacher, "we could never have taken a load like that."

With headquarters in a quaint red-brick building in Trenton's Mill Hill section, Mercer Street Friends was established in 1956 by Quakers pursuant to their fundamental mission to promote tolerance and social justice. The organization's service spectrum ranges from job counseling, life-skills training and educational tutoring for adults to full day-care and after-school programs for hundreds of children to the provision of skilled health-care for the homebound elderly and disabled. By dint of sheer growth, though, the regional food bank more or less has become a focal point and an emblem of the organization's overall efforts. Starting in the early 1980s—again, the same shared time-frame with TASK and the Community FoodBank of New Jersey—the Mercer Street Friends operation began as a network of small pantries and now supplies enough food to reach more than 16,000 people in need every month. Nutrition workshops and cooking demonstrations staged by MSF personnel and volunteers provide training in proper food handling, storage and safety techniques, menu planning and preparation for cooks and other workers at the organization's client charities. The group also has been a leader in advocacy and outreach, particularly in shepherding low-income individuals and families through the tangled and often-confusing maze of social assistance programs, such as food stamps, for which they may be eligible but not know it.

Fastidious and focused, with the distinct aspect about her of someone used to juggling several problems at once and changing direction quickly as circumstances warrant, Stoolmacher joined Mercer Street Friends about 20 years ago and has seen the food operation evolve from an *ad hoc* emergency outlet to the well-oiled machinery of hunger-industry commerce. Every day, like a shipping expediter in any sort of industrial warehouse, she works the phones, tracking the needs of client agencies, finding out what's available across the marketplace, cutting deals with independent food brokers around the region who are looking to unload odd lots of canned meat, pasta, juice or other commodities that were over-ordered or otherwise unwanted by their regular commercial customers. "We buy in volume—200 cases of this, 200 cases of that," she says. "We'll then give it to our agencies either for free or at very low cost. Basically, we charge a shared maintenance fee—18 cents a pound—to cover some of the handling and distribution charges at our end. It doesn't matter what the food's retail value is; it's based on the weight. Our role is to get the food out of here as fast as we can, and the reason food banks are so critical is that we can provide a consistent supply throughout the year. It's a reliable supply of food at a low cost, and those things enable our agencies to plan and to devote scarce dollars to other services."

One of the most striking, albeit mundane, characteristics of Hunger, Inc., at any level is the volume of paperwork it entails. Filed or piled somewhere is a typed or hand-written configuration for use in everything from tracking inventory to maintaining spreadsheets detailing revenues and expenditures to compiling reports analyzing data on the changing shape of client needs. Indeed, Stoolmacher's desktop is blanketed in a veritable mini-bureaucracy of paper, including what arguably is the most critical link in the charitable food-service chain—forms used by client agencies to place orders. Leafing through one pile, Stoolmacher pulls out a recent order faxed over from TASK for 50 cases of spaghetti sauce, 10 of rice, and 20 each of elbow macaroni, Ramen Noodles and canned green beans. At the bottom, a hand-scrawled note says, "Phyllis, any possibility of getting meat for us?" Considerable time and energy are also spent making sure the food winds up where it's supposed to, that it's handled properly and that it comprises an appropriate mix for the various agencies that receive it. "We make site visits annually and check on storage, security, those sorts of things," Stoolmacher says. They'll even take the temperature inside refrigerators and freezers to minimize risk of spoilage—all part of the obligation and operational profile of a going concern.

From time to time, Stoolmacher contemplates whether circumstances will ever arrange themselves in such a way as to finally put the thriving business of which Mercer Street Friends is a part out of business. "Even if that were to happen, I think we'd still have the issue of food that needs to be recycled," she observes. "But do I wish I didn't have to do this because people are hungry? Absolutely. You kind of get disillusioned after a while. The problem's getting worse, not better."

•   •   •

Shopping day: it's already been a busy one for Tom Reilly, the man behind the wheel of TASK's delivery van. The morning brought the usual round of visits to area bakeries and stores for leftover pastries, bagels, donuts, pies and cakes, then the noon-hour stop at Whole Foods where he and helper who goes by the name of Lloyd collected bread, fresh vegetables and produce, some of it, like the kiwi fruits and oddly-shaped mushrooms, looking rather exotic considering their destination. Now, as Tom eases the van in reverse up to the edge of the Mercer Street Friends loading area, a volunteer materializes from the depths of the warehouse to greet him with a clipboard bearing the soup kitchen's confirmed biweekly order. Another food bank worker maneuvers a mechanical cart across the floor, and, with Tom and Lloyd trailing behind, the small entourage makes its way down the aisle, stopping from time to time to hoist bulk loads of groceries: seven shrink-wrapped crates of canned sliced beef with gravy; a dozen 15-jar boxes of spaghetti with meatballs; six bundles of long grain rice, each containing 12 two-pound bags; three boxes of one-pound margarine blocks; a dozen large cartons of vegetable oil; and, finally, from the freezer, 16 20-pound boxes of chicken tenders.

Tom swings open the van's rear double doors, and as he and Lloyd begin hefting the order inside, Phyllis Stoolmacher steps up to announce the food bank's version of a daily shoppers' special: fresh potatoes, onions, apples and lettuce—all free for the taking today because they need to be moved and moved quickly. Tom's eyes light up at the offer. "Don't look a gift horse in the mouth," he says, hauling off two big bags of the complimentary onions and four banana boxes full of potatoes. By now, the van is listing noticeably on the driver's side.

"That's not so bad," Tom says with a laugh. "One time we left here so loaded the tires were almost flat."

He opens the door, but before climbing inside, shouts a loud "Thank you, Phyllis!" Comes the reply from somewhere amid the pallets, "You're welcome. Enjoy!'

4

Faces in the Crowd

If you walk into the Trenton Area Soup Kitchen with preconceived notions of who's who, you should be prepared to have your mind blown—figuratively speaking, that is. For example, about that thirtysomething white guy over there, the one wearing a silver ear stud, fashionably baggy shorts and a polo shirt adorned with a logo that says "Makefield Highlands Golf Club." What's he doing here? Must be someone helping out, probably a volunteer. And that black woman seated nearby, the one talking and laughing and gesturing with people as they join the food-service line? Definitely someone in need.

Wrong on both counts.

In fact, it's just the opposite. The well-dressed fellow who looks like he could be your golfing buddy is a recovering crack-cocaine addict who came to TASK just a few weeks ago because he was homeless and had no place to go. After wandering the streets, he stumbled upon the soup kitchen where he not only found food but also clothing (except for the ear stud, of course) and guidance in navigating the social-services bureaucracy. He told me he was trying, without much luck so far, to find a job in construction with the goal of getting an apartment. "I just need some help," he said. And the woman? She's a soup kitchen employee whose job includes distributing meal tickets. Her personality simply lends itself to animated conversation and good cheer, and she tries to exchange words of greeting with everyone who comes her way.

Stereotypes. Better to leave them on the doorstep, especially when it comes to the patron population.

To be sure, the soup kitchen draws its share of run-of-the-mill down-and-outers, those lost souls everyone used to refer to as vagrants and derelicts, indeed the profile many people still associate with such places, viewed from a distance, as they often are, as little more than the offspring of Depression-era bread lines. But the demographic of need has changed drastically in just the last few decades, and that change is plain at TASK every day. The crowds are larger, and they are younger. While faces of color predominate, they are merely part of a racial quilt that includes a fair number of Caucasians and, in a reflection of recent immigration trends, rising numbers of people of Hispanic heritage. There are more women and children, especially during the summer when school is out, and, strikingly, nearly one-third of TASK's patrons are people who have jobs but don't get paid enough to make ends meet. The conditions giving rise to the need have changed as well, founded, of course, in basic economic poverty but fueled dramatically now by a potent mixture of complex social problems that seem to defy solution—unceasing drug abuse, violence, family disintegration, poor education and a universe of protracted mental disorders.

Under other circumstances and in other places, battling back against obstacles of such magnitude might be considered exceptional. At TASK, it happens all the time. And if you ever go there, you might want to consider these stories, the stories behind three faces in the soup kitchen crowd.

•

Against All Odds

Ray never had much use for faith, or luck for that matter. Growing up in a rough section of south Trenton, he learned at an early age to rely on a somewhat more tangible set of tools to get through the day, starting with fists and quick reflexes. That's what really put you in control. The rest was for losers.

But now here he was, alone at a desk, getting ready to confront something that threatened to render his street-wise self-reliance utterly powerless. Ray was in the middle of a test, literally, the final exam for a Graduate Equivalency Diploma. He'd made it through the barrage of science, social studies, math and English questions, seemingly without a hitch, but now came the hard part: the written essay. He would have to compose at least five paragraphs, the minimum requirement, and he was petrified. Despite months of tutoring and instruction, practice and concentration, he continued to wrestle anxiously with the effects of dyslexia—spelling mix-ups, trouble stringing words together in the proper order. He also knew that GED exam booklets present essay topics at random, and dark thoughts about the result of that sort of roulette abruptly crossed his mind: What if it's something I don't know much about? What if I can't think of anything to write? What if I run out of time? What if …?

He turned the page—and breathed a sigh of relief.

"The question was something like, 'What's been the biggest accomplishment in your life?'" he recalls. "I wrote about getting clean from alcohol and drugs. It was what I knew, and so I was freely writing and I wasn't stuck on anything. The words were just coming out, coming out, and I was just writing and writing."

Ray passed that test, nailed it in fact, scoring above the 90th percentile. In the process, he also became, at 24, one of the most celebrated students in the history of the TASK's adult education program, completing his studies and earning a GED in just four months—a record for the organization.

How does he explain it now? Partly, like this: "God blessed me on that one, man. He gave me something that he knew I could write about."

•   •   •

When he was five years old, his father walked away from home and never came back. This was on Power Street, an ironically named spit of row houses across Route 29 from an old industrial site now occupied by Waterfront Park. "I have no picture of him, nothing. The only characteristic I remember is that he was missing a thumb. He could walk past me right now and I wouldn't even know him." He left behind a wife on disability and four children—Ray, an older sister and twin younger brothers, all close in age. He says his mother did the best she could under the circumstances. They were clothed properly and never ran short of food. Every Christmas, she saved enough for a decorated tree and took the kids on a special excursion to K-Mart where each could choose what $15 would buy. Ray remembers picking PowerRangers and Teenage Mutant Ninja Turtles. "Looking back, I realize why she had to do that, but at the time it was hard because other kids were getting this and getting this and getting this. I remember one Christmas morning when me and my brothers walked around the neighborhood and picked up old toys that were thrown out. That was a good Christmas when we did that. We made our own fun."

Mostly, though, it wasn't fun.

"We were the only white kids in the neighborhood," he recalls. "In elementary school, it was only us three boys, so you can imagine the fights we got into. I was always hurt because of the fighting, and I missed a lot of school." When he was nine, someone bashed him from behind with a length of pipe. The assault put him in a coma and left him with a permanent lump on the back of his head, but that wasn't the half of it: Ray had been diagnosed with hemophilia, a genetic disorder marked by the body's inability to stop hemorrhaging, and doctors were concerned for his life. He recovered, but the incident was one of a series that finally prompted intervention by social-service authorities. The New Jersey Division of Youth and Family Services (DYFS) assigned a counselor and eventually assisted the family in moving to another location, a house on Beatty Street about a mile away. There was less conflict on the streets, but in school, Ray fell apart. He was 13.

"I was so far behind by the time I got to seventh grade they had to put me in special education. I couldn't write at all. I couldn't spell anything." Oddly, he posted impressive scores on standardized tests. "My reading level was through the roof, and I excelled at math, but for some reason, I just couldn't grasp spelling. It just wouldn't work." But no one connected the dots, and Ray came to feel like he was put in a corner and left there. He still marvels at the fact that he continued to be promoted. Apart from his classroom struggles, there was his medical condition, "my blood disorder," he says, "and everybody always had to know about it, the teachers and all. So they always treated me differently, like I had a disease, you know, like 'don't play with him.' It just went downhill from there." By the ripe age of 15, he'd had enough. The precipitating event was a hallway fight at Trenton High School. "On my third day in ninth grade, I got into a scuffle with another kid over cigarettes. He called me a fucking liar and punched me in the face. I said, 'I can't deal with this shit no more,' and I ran home and never went back."

At the time, Ray was also well beyond experimenting with drugs. He didn't much care for marijuana and "the fuzzy feeling it gave me," but alcohol was a different matter entirely. "When I was 14, I was at my friend's house and he was like, 'Yo, I got some liquor from my dad, you want take a couple of shots? I took three shots of a liquor called Jagermeister, and that was it. Looking back, I realize now that I was an alcoholic from that point on. I remember those three shots. I remember how that made me feel, and I distinctly remember telling myself as I walked home, 'This is how I want to feel the rest of my life, all the time.' It gave me a sense of security. It took away the fear of walking down the street and getting beat up. It took away the insecurity of talking to people, the insecurity of talking to girls. I mean, it took all that away instantly. The next day I was out looking for more."

Against this backdrop, things came unglued pretty quickly. Ray and a few pals spent their days trolling the city's "bum huts" to recruit and pay homeless people to buy liquor for them. Meanwhile, school authorities came after him for chronic truancy, and his mother, as legal guardian, was hit with fines until a plan was worked out to enroll him in an alternate school for children with handicaps and disabilities. For a while, things seemed to stabilize. "I really loved that school," Ray says. "It was small, and I felt like I fit in. I didn't feel ashamed to raise my hand and say I didn't know this or that, because the other kids didn't know it either." But it didn't stop his behavior from spiraling out of control. One day, he and a couple of friends stole and crashed a car and landed in jail, and in Ray's case, it was a watershed event: DYFS intervened again, this time launching him into a blur of rehab and related facilities, in effect making him a ward of the state. Soon he learned his brothers were on the road to a similar fate; in fact, it seemed like a grenade had gone off in the family, flinging male bodies in every direction. One of the twins took the worst of it, winding up in a psychiatric institution. Only later would Ray learn that a key part of the whole ugly equation was the fact that a social-service "youth advocate" had sexually molested both of his brothers beginning before they were ten years old. The man, a serial child predator, was eventually arrested, convicted and sent to prison.

At 17, Ray was transferred to a residential counseling program in Somerset County, about 40 miles northwest of Trenton. The program required him to enroll in the local public high school, and, once again, a spark of intellect flashed in spite of himself and what he had been through. Although he continued to trip over the fundamentals of spelling, teachers found that he could read at close to a college level. More telling, he was placed in a gifted and talented science class and entered vocational training as an apprentice electrician with the prospect of a job with AT&T. But it didn't last. "Here I was 17 years old, still in ninth grade, and I fell in with the wrong crowd again. As a result, basically I got re-educated into drugs, and not just pot and alcohol, but stuff like Vicodin, Percocet, ecstasy, acid, ketamine—all of it." In November 1999, his mother was diagnosed with lung cancer. She died two months later, and shortly thereafter, Ray—now over 18 and beyond the reach of child-welfare authorities—dropped out of the Somerset program and returned to Trenton. He calls that move "the worst mistake of my life."

Initially, things were looking up. One of his brothers was back on his feet and getting ready to enlist in the Navy. Ray thought about that and concluded it might be a good fit for him, too. But as the recruiter went through the routine questions about medical history, it quickly became clear that hemophilia was an insurmountable disqualifier. Instead, he took a job slinging fast food at a Roy Rodgers in the Trenton train station. In the meantime, he discovered the peculiarly enticing and dangerously addicting qualities of crack cocaine. Ray had always been reluctant to add what is known on the street as "rock" to his substance-abuse collection because he thought it had to be melted through some elaborate process called free-basing and wasn't worth the trouble. "But I met this guy who told me you could put it in a joint with marijuana and smoke it. For me, eventually it became less and less weed and more and more crack, to the point where it was all crack and no weed."

He stopped going to work but found a means to stay in the money by using his medical condition to qualify for a monthly check under the federal Supplemental Security Income (SSI) program for persons with disabilities. Then he stopped paying rent, and with the dawn of the new year in 2003, Ray was homeless—and, in what he describes as his "addict's mind," he couldn't have cared less. "I had a system down," he says. "I'd buy me a 'forty' (a 40-ounce bottle of beer), a half-pint of liquor, a nickel bag of weed and a $10 rock and go hang out in a park. I'd be fucked up all day." As for living arrangements, he joined the ranks of other dissolute souls in the city who trudge through a daily circuit of stops along what has come to be known in local anti-poverty circles as "the Trenton Triangle." They spend their nights in the Rescue Mission just off Perry Street. At 8 a.m., when they are rousted out for the day, many head in the direction of a "drop-in" center on East State Street maintained by the Salvation Army. There, they kill time until 10:30 or so when TASK opens its doors over on Escher Street. As far as Ray and his "system" were concerned, the soup kitchen was the critical link. "It gave me something to eat at least once a day."

•   •   •

He doesn't remember the exact moment he decided "get clean." There was no flash of clarity, no grand epiphany that some former addicts describe. Maybe it was pressure from people at the Rescue Mission who were telling him that after eight months, he had overstayed his welcome. Maybe he just got sick and tired of feeling sick and tired. Maybe it was something deeper. In any event, one day in 2004 he tried being sober and wound up scaring the daylights out of himself. "I made it about a day, and I started to shake. Then I started to get cold sweats and shit. I didn't know what was going on. So I went to talk to a friend of mine and he tells me I'm having the DTs." Ray's first instinct was to find something to take off the edge, which is what he did. But that disturbing taste of withdrawal continued to rattle around his head, and so he talked things over with someone at a drug-abuse treatment center and wound up in detox at a rehabilitation center in Princeton. Forty-five days later, he was placed in monitored transitional housing back in Trenton, a single-room occupancy (SRO) structure located just down Escher Street from TASK. That's when he learned that the soup kitchen wasn't just a soup kitchen, that it also offered an array of social-service programs, including instruction towards a GED.

"At first, I just chilled, didn't apply myself," he says. But, once again, in spite of himself, that flash of underlying intellect would not be denied. A routine intake evaluation by TASK's adult education coordinator, Kelly Hansen, crackled with potential. "She said right from the start that it was only going to take about eight months to get my GED. She was like, 'You can do better, Ray. I don't know why you won't push yourself. You're better than this.'"

In the end, her estimate was off by half. It took only four months.

With his GED in hand by the end of 2004, Ray started scouting around for a job, volunteering as a tutor at TASK in the meantime while staying at the SRO. His break came a few months later when the director of transitional housing there offered him a part-time job watching over and counseling occupants on weekends. He also enrolled at Mercer County Community College on a Pell grant, aiming at first for a degree in computer systems and network administration but, after one semester, completely changing gears to concentrate on social work. Why the switch? "What I've been through made me who I am," he says. "It made me able to help others. A lot of people who come into social work and the human services are educated through books. I'm educated through experience. So when I'm talking to these people I know exactly what they're going through. I know all the agencies, I know how to get around the obstacles, I know what's available."

·   ·   ·

I met Ray when the worst of this was behind him. It was a hot day in mid-June 2006, and he was standing on the sidewalk outside his new home, a north Trenton apartment he was sharing with one of his brothers. Dressed in an over-sized basketball jersey and baggy jeans, he looked like any other gangly twentysomething ready to chase the day. Though he walks with a bit of limp and finds it difficult to extend his right arm for a handshake—the long-term effects of hemophilia on the body's limbs and joints—he told me he was getting decent medical care and his job responsibilities were about to expand. He was also looking forward with no small measure of excitement to his first-ever proper vacation: a train trip to Niagara Falls, coming up in just a few weeks.

He climbed into my car (he was still working toward his own set of wheels), and we drove over to TASK where he talked virtually nonstop into a tape recorder for an hour and a half. In his spare time, he said, he still tries to do some tutoring. He remembers what it did for him. "It was the confidence factor," he said. "They were always reassuring me, telling me I'm not stupid, that I can do this, that I know what I can excel at so why not take that and run with it instead of focusing on the negatives of learning like why I can't spell so well. They said, 'Let's just put that aside for now and get to the rest of it.'

"I'm still a very big part of this soup kitchen," he added, motioning at the building and the people around him. "This place really damn near saved my life."

·

Los Trabajadores de Bajos Ingresos

It's the last week of the month, and with rent coming due on top of other bills that already have consumed most of his latest paycheck, Luis has little choice in the matter: if he wants a decent hot meal, one he can afford, the soup kitchen is pretty much the only game in town. "I don't come here every day," he says. "But sometimes, like near the end of the month when there's not enough money left and I'm running out of food and struggling big time, this place helps me."

Trabajadores de Bajos Ingresos (Trah-ba-ha-DOR-es Dey BAH-hose In-GRAY-sos) is Spanish for "workers with low wages." More to the point, it means "the working poor," which, in any language, is a world-class contradiction in terms. But it is a condition nevertheless exemplified by Luis and many others these days who find it impossible to keep up with basic necessities despite tethering themselves to one, two or even three jobs at the minimum wage or better. On any given day, you see them moving through the line at TASK, some in slacks or dress shirts, others in construction coveralls, their oil-stained and calloused fingers gripping special tickets that guarantee quick meal service so they can be back to work by the end of their allotted lunch hour. The soup kitchen started offering these "express" passes on an organized basis several years ago when it became apparent that working men and women were beginning to comprise a regular, identifiable and growing segment of its overall patron population. Area food pantries and other outlets for emergency provisions have noted the same phenomenon tugging at their services. "It used to be mostly the unemployed, a lot of homeless, but today it's also working people, many with families," says Phyllis Stoolmacher, director of the Mercer Street Friends Food Bank. "They live paycheck to paycheck, and when they run out of money, they give up buying food. They pay the rent because they don't want to become homeless." At HomeFront, in suburban Lawrenceville, demand for emergency food is rising at a rate of 20 percent a year, propelled in part by the ranks of the working poor. "Each and every day we have folks who come in, and the look on their face tells you the story that they never thought they'd be in a place like this," says Connie Mercer, the organization's director. "They never thought they'd be the ones asking for a handout. Some will tell us that last year, they contributed food to us. And they're ashamed. But somehow they have to feed their family." Though the faces in HomeFront's waiting area on any given day are predominantly black, Mercer says the agency routinely sees the entire racial spectrum, with increasing numbers of Hispanics.

Similarly, in South Trenton, where TASK has established a small adjunct soup kitchen in a working-class neighborhood, clutches of Hispanic men and women, some with children in tow, can be observed on weekday evenings stepping through the doors of the First Baptist Church on Center Street. On the way in, they pass a banner tied to the wrought-iron fence out front that says, "South Trenton Cocina—Se Sirven Comidas Calientes—Lunes, Miercoles y Jueves." Gathering in a large multi-purpose room adjacent to the sanctuary, some settle into seats at cloth-covered tables and start eating while others take their supper across the room to a table manned by volunteers who wrap the food-laden trays to take home. Above the sound of footsteps and the rustle of cellophane and plastic bags, a low murmur of accented conversation filters through the air. Little English is spoken here, and most keep to themselves. Although the South Trenton Cocina now draws small crowds on a regular basis, organizers say it was difficult getting the operation up and running. Initially, despite obvious need in the surrounding community, people shied away because of the cultural stigma associated with having to turn to others for help—especially in a non-Catholic religious setting—and, in some instances, out of fear that authorities might question their immigration status.

Likewise, outside TASK's main building on Escher Street on the other side of town, it is not unusual to find small groups of young, predominantly Hispanic men seated on benches or milling about in casual conversation. They are from Mexico, Honduras, Guatemala and other points south, and they speak of living together in cramped apartments, of waiting on street corners of the city to be picked up after dawn by vans or other vehicles that take them to landscaping, excavation or construction jobs, of wiring part of the $50 or $60 cash they receive for a day's work back home. If you ask, they will tell you in no uncertain terms that they are here legally. But no credentials are volunteered, no green cards displayed, and their voices abruptly trail off into another topic for a minute or two before they walk away.

In some key respects, Luis is advantageously atypical of his work-a-day soup kitchen compadres. For one thing, he is a U.S. citizen, born and raised in Trenton, the son of parents who came from Puerto Rico. He has a high school diploma, speaks fluent English and is pretty well steeped in what you need to do to survive on the mean streets of a gang-plagued American city. He also makes a good deal more than the mini-mum wage—$11.35 an hour—and has a steady job, with benefits, load-ing and unloading trucks at a huge warehouse owned by The Sports Authority in a rural community bisected by I-295 a dozen or so miles southwest of Trenton. Even so, Luis has found that what adds up to a weekly paycheck, before taxes, of $425 erodes quickly against the pres-sure of $650 a month for a studio apartment, plus food, clothing, trans-portation—no car, but $50 a month for the RiverLine light rail to and from work—and assorted incidentals like basic cable T.V. A couple of years ago, in an effort to put some space between himself and the bill collectors, Luis took a second job three nights a week doing similar unskilled labor at a Sav-A-lot bulk grocery outlet. Still, there are days when the string runs out, and he joins the line at the soup kitchen.

"It's tough, but you gotta do what you gotta do," he says. "I go to work, pay my bills, take it as it is. Every day."

•   •   •

He is the first to admit to a series of missteps and wrong turns taken early in his 42 years on the planet, conscious choices that helped put him where he is today. Raised in a Christian Pentecostal household, the youngest of four children, Luis says he grew up feeling smothered by rigid religious strictures enforced by his parents. He rebelled. At 17, he got involved with a girl a year younger, and she became pregnant. "There was no love, but I felt I had to take care of her," he says. This was in the early 80s, and he took jobs washing dishes during the day, cleaning offices at night. Two years later, she was pregnant again. "Like I say, when I was young, I made mistakes."

After about five years of grinding out menial paydays, Luis decided to chase an opportunity. He moved to New York City at the invitation of his older brother, who had started his own family there after settling into a career as a catering chef. But, again, Luis sabotaged himself. Working by day in the kitchen of the Marriott Hotel on 57th Street, he hung out at night selling drugs, mostly marijuana. "I could make maybe $200 from after work until midnight," he says. But one evening in 1988 the easy money abruptly dried up. Busted by the police, Luis was convicted and sentenced to four years in jail, two of which he spent in the harrowing cellblocks of Rikers Island, birthplace of a criminal gang known as the Latin Kings. Initially established as a secret, prison-based self-protective association for Latino inmates, the Latin Kings exercised a powerful attraction, and Luis was among those who joined. He still bears an indelible mark of that membership, a small bluish tattoo shaped like a tear immediately below and to the left of his right eye. It was applied using the distinctly unconventional means of a sharpened staple and a prison-concocted dye consisting of ballpoint-pen ink and candle soot.

Paroled two years later, Luis gravitated back to the Trenton area with no job and no place to live, and he wound up in an emergency shelter. Today, he looks back at the daunting week he spent there as his own personal "scared straight" experience and thinks it probably saved his life. "It was like jail," he says. "You eat when they tell you to eat, what they give you to eat. You got people coming at you fighting. They steal—even your underwear. You wash your dirty underwear and hang them by your bed, and the next morning you find somebody else's dirty underwear there. The only good thing about it was you could leave when you wanted to leave, and I did everything I could to get out of there and stay out of there."

He signed on with a large temporary employment agency that specializes in placing workers, as needed, in commercial warehouses operated by chain super-stores. Most days, a slot was found for Luis, but it soon became obvious that the pay scale at the time, $8 an hour, was insufficient to cover living expenses, and so he took part-time evening jobs, first at McDonalds, then Kentucky Fried Chicken. The one salutary aspect of the warehouse situation, however, was that he received training as a forklift operator, and, after four months of day-by-day temporary work, was qualified to apply for a full-time position at slightly higher pay, plus limited benefits.

·   ·   ·

Besides a tight budget, Luis' work schedule generally leaves him little time to prepare meals other than quick-fix items like hotdogs or frozen pizza—nothing close to the variety and nutritional balance available at TASK. The soup kitchen has also introduced an element of social structure into his life, and on the evenings he turns up for a meal there, he's found that an hour or two spent in the company of others is worth the daunting trip he faces on the way home. It's a 45-minute walk—"maybe 35, if I walk fast"—to his apartment just over the city line in suburban Hamilton Township, and getting there means covering ground in parts of the city many fear to tread even in broad daylight. "I been chased, stuck up," he says. "There's a point, sort of a border I cross where I feel safe. But after 10 o'clock, I know I don't have no business out there." He's thought about moving closer in, maybe joining a group of other day-laborers in a rent-pooling arrangement that would reduce expenses. A couple guys he knows joined a dozen others in renting a two-bedroom house where they each pay $85 a month. Despite the obvious savings, though it's not for him. "No privacy," Luis says. "I need my space."

Eventually, he hopes to save enough for a car but beyond that, "I have no idea what I want to do. I've come a long way. I don't get in trouble no more. But I don't know. To be honest with you, I'm just surviving right now."

•

The Long Way Home

By her own account, Ann got swept up in some colossal episodes of self-destructive behavior during what she calls her "out-of-control" years. But looking back over the whole ugly trail—the drug abuse, the thievery, the abandonment of her children, homelessness, prison—she says the stunt most heavily freighted with potential disaster may well have been a simple spur-of-the-moment confrontation that occurred one day inside the soup kitchen. "I got into a loud argument with some girl who owed me five dollars, and they almost threw me out. It was stupid, really silly." Only later would she come to realize that "silly" did not begin to define the possible consequences of that incident. Not only would she have lost a meal ticket, which she desperately needed at the time, but over the long run, getting tossed from TASK would have proved to be tantamount to taking a flying leap from a bridge. That's because the place not only gave her food, "but the people who volunteer here, the people who work here, they gave me hope." And that, she says, helped put her on the road to recovery and self-sufficiency.

Today, Ann is an AmeriCorps/VISTA volunteer and founder of a small nonprofit social-service agency that serves as a sort of clearing-house for information about employment opportunities, education and training programs, housing and rental assistance, the availability of food, clothing and other basic necessities. Working out of a cramped studio apartment in Trenton's Mill Hill section, piles of paperwork and donated computer equipment sharing space with a fold-down Murphy bed and a few other pieces of furniture, she stitches together weekly newsletters and bulletins and sends them by e-mail to some 1,500 recipients across the state—churches, advocacy groups, government agencies, individuals. For those without access to computers, she cranks out hard copies with a worn Hewlett-Packard printer and hands them out on the street. "A lot of people who are trying to get on their feet think there's nothing they can do, but actually there's a lot they can do," she says. "I've been down the road of homelessness, down that bad road, and I try to give them hope from the experience of where I've come from." TASK, which offers patrons free access to a bank of PCs in its computer room, was among the first facilities she contacted about posting the information she collects. "This place was here for me when I was out there," she explains. "They cared about me when I didn't even care about me."

·   ·   ·

If logic were the sole arbiter of how a life unfolds, things likely would have turned quite differently for this stocky, brown-haired woman who was orphaned at birth and who struggled for years against a haunting sense of abandonment. She was put up for adoption as an infant and remembers little in the way of joy during a childhood spent in the rigid confines of a cold and troubled household in Trenton's far south end. When she speaks of those years in the 60s, it is like hearing about a shadow world, and when the subject turns to the couple who took her in, she hesitates. "The woman—I still have a hard time referring to her as my mother—she was a very abusive person." There were beatings, she says, and they happened in a way that had to be obvious to adult relatives who behaved as if nothing were wrong. "Not long ago," Ann says, "I ran into my aunt and uncle on my [adoptive] father's side. I was going by their house, and I had to stop. I felt I had to see them, talk to them. We had a long talk, and I asked about the bruises and the other stuff, and they acknowledged knowing about those things. But they said they couldn't do anything."

She started drinking alcohol, she guesses, "when I was like nine years old" and drank pretty much all the way through high school and beyond. "When I was working, I can barely remember a time when I came home early before the bars closed." At 19, she met a man, and they married. A year later, she gave birth to a daughter. It would be the first of seven marriages, and the first of four children—each by a different father. No excuses, she says. "Just irresponsible."

In the late 80s, Ann moved to Florida where she spent the better part of a decade "meandering all over the place." Cocaine entered her life. "You could get it anywhere," she says. "Until about 1999, I held it together, but I was really drinking and drugging, and I wasn't paying the bills. Then, one day—and I don't know why, it just came out of my mouth—I said I was going to do something to my children. And somebody intervened and called the authorities and child welfare came and took my children, and I just went on my way." Heading north, she wound up back in New Jersey, drifted into Trenton and spent much of her time "walking the streets—I was a street girl." It was at this point that she became acquainted with, and, because of that five-dollar altercation, nearly got thrown out of, the soup kitchen. "I came for food, clothing, hygiene products. It gave me a break from being out there." But it didn't stop her from committing what she herself describes as an astonishing act of betrayal. Sometime in 2001, she contrived a plan to get her hands on some easy money by raiding a bank account established for her eldest daughter, who still lived in the city. Five years after the fact, Ann closes her eyes and swallows hard. "I took her identity," she says, "and I took her trust fund, and I went on the run."

She roamed the country for nearly two years, going city to city, crashing in public shelters, sometimes sleeping under bridges on a journey that sounds like some sad, trite country and western ballad. In Nashville, she says, she met a long-haul truck driver "who took me under his wing. He just thought maybe I had a hard life, and he was someone who genuinely cared about me, and I told him the truth." During this period, she also found herself slowly losing a taste for drugs. "Something happened," she says. "It was like there was a change happening, like I was hearing and understanding more about life." Part of it was the fact that, depending on where she was, she would spend time in public libraries, reading and fiddling with computers and the Internet. At one point—she thinks it was in Sacramento—she took it upon herself to research local job and housing options, and she started passing along the information to needy acquaintances: a rough early seedling of the nonprofit she would later establish, though she didn't know it at the time. And there was something else going on. Ann does not describe herself as "born again"; it didn't happen that way. But over time, she found herself leaning more and more heavily on religious faith, and one day she gathered the courage for a decision that she says was inspired, in part, from above. Reaching out to someone she knew back in New Jersey, an attorney, she found that there was an outstanding warrant for her arrest. "It was time," she says, and so she turned herself in

In the end, after the extradition waiver and all the other court proceedings were dispensed with and the final gavel came down, Ann served ten months in the minimum-security Edna Mahon Correctional Center in rural Clinton, N.J. "I did what I was supposed to there," she says, "and I felt happy not to have to look over my shoulder anymore." Before long, she was selected to chair meetings of the prison's Alcoholics Anonymous group, an experience she looks back upon as having been "a privilege." In July 2004, she was released "with a better understanding about my disease"—but little else. Returning once again to Trenton, she immediately confronted a harsh reality that often awaits prison inmates freshly paroled: no job, no income, no place to spend the night except outdoors or inside the city's Rescue Mission, which is located in a drug-infested zone along Carroll and Perry streets. Ann opted for the latter even though "it scared me to death to be back on those streets. That's the same place I used to do my bad stuff." Lucky for her, a change of address was soon in coming, and she was placed in single-room-occupancy transitional housing down the street from TASK. The facility's proximity to the soup kitchen proved fortuitous. Not only did it provide a convenient source of nutrition while she pulled together the wherewithal to do her own cooking, but she could also take advantage of free classes to burnish her computer skills. And that was the essential part. For the first time in her checkered life, she saw the future and had a sensible plan for reaching it.

•   •   •

One morning not long ago, as Ann contemplated the approach of her 46th birthday and the third year of nurturing her self-created nonprofit agency for the homeless and unemployed, she spoke of days filled with phone calls and chores that keep her in front of her computer terminal late into the night.

"For now, "I'm on my own," she said, smiling, letting the words sink in. "I love my life today." At the same time, she was preparing for some significant changes. Three of her four children remained in Florida, and her top priority was to do everything necessary "to re-connect with them." Also, new responsibilities loomed as an AmeriCorps/VISTA volunteer for which she would receive a monthly stipend of $900—earnings she expected would put her on a path out of welfare and off of food stamps. Meanwhile, her fledgling information clearing-house had grown to a point where she had little choice but to start solic-iting partnerships with other agencies and devising strategies to raise funds. "I get phone calls all times of the day and night," she said. "And it's not just those you might expect. At this point in time, it's everybody. I'm hearing from people who were laid off a while ago from big compa-nies, people who have run out of their severance" and exhausted the usual job-search channels.

But even amid that broadening mix of need, much of her time was still devoted to the particularly tangled plight of ex-offenders. Having experienced her own chilling sense of free-fall upon release from prison, Ann said they face "a huge challenge" in securing adequate housing and decent employment, and every bit of progress must be measured a victory. In one instance, she helped a parolee find work at a gas station. "After six months," she said, "he's still got a job and now he has benefits." In another, she helped find an apartment for a woman "within 10 days of her release. She already had a job but no paycheck yet for housing."

But no matter who enlists her service, Ann said, her approach is always the same: "To show those who are still out there that it can be done.... For me to be here today doing the work I do, this is it. This is my home city and coming back here to live my life right, I think that's awesome."

5

The Spirit of TASK

G rowing up in a small town in Iowa, Jamie Murphy could hardly have imagined that one day she would find herself halfway across the country in a New Jersey soup kitchen handing out food to bedraggled strangers. Or that some of those same strangers would return her smile and thank her. Or that she would talk to them, get to know them, make friends.

But it all happened one spring, the spring of her senior year at Rider University.

Like other college students in the greater Trenton area, Jamie decided to fulfill a requisite semester internship by volunteering several days a week at TASK. At first, she was apprehensive, not quite sure what to expect. She'd heard stories about the city. "People warned me it was in a bad neighborhood, that I shouldn't take or wear anything expensive. I was afraid I'd go that first day and not want to go back. But I didn't have that experience at all. I actually kind of enjoyed it." So much so that as graduation approached, she started thinking about how to arrange her schedule so she could continue volunteering through the summer. "One thing I'm going to take away from this is that these people's lives are so rough, much rougher than mine, but when you talk to some of them they seem to have a better outlook. I mean, if I were in their position, having to come to a soup kitchen to eat every day, I think I'd be whole lot more angry at life than they seem to be. It really puts things in perspective."

Her experience is at once emblematic and exceptional when it comes to the profile of volunteerism at TASK. The organization boasts a prodigious record of nurturing and maintaining a loyal volunteer corps that today numbers some 780 individuals—an unusually deep and sustaining foundation of hands-on support for a nonprofit organization of modest size. Most of these folks, of course, reside in Trenton and surrounding communities and don't have to travel nearly as far to get there as, say, a coed from the Midwest. And they do it for all sorts of reasons apart from gaining academic credit: to give back, to stay busy, to do something interesting, to fulfill their own need, to simply help those less fortunate.

Regardless of motivation or starting point, they are on a common journey. These are the stories of three who have taken that journey to places that exemplify the spirit of TASK.

•

The Utility Infielder

Seated at the wheel of TASK's delivery van one afternoon, Tom Reilly was sorting through a batch of paperwork when a thick white envelope fell into his lap. Inside, he found a Christmas card signed "Shorty"—the nickname of a longtime soup kitchen regular he had befriended. The card brought a smile. But then he took a closer look at the envelope, and his smile gave way to a deep chuckle. On it, in big block letters, Shorty had written, "To: Tom (Santa Claus)."

There's a good reason for Shorty's choice of that particular parenthetic alias, and it is a source of never-ending amusement in and around TASK. Reilly happens to be the very spitting image of the old boy, even in short sleeves and khakis: shock of grayish-white hair, thick brows, full white beard—all genuine. So, too, the spectacles. And the eyes—there's definitely a gleam if not an outright twinkle. And, of course, the signature girth and build, though no where near mythic proportions. Red-suited and fully booked every year between Thanksgiving and Christmas, he *is* Santa, appearing in all sorts of venues to the delight of children and adults alike. He laughs every time he thinks about it. "Even my wife's been sucked into playing Mrs. Claus," he says. "It's fun."

That's because it happens to be a perfect fit. In a world that all too often resembles a roaring, rushing train fueled by ambition, material gain and self-aggrandizement, Tom Reilly is the guy who got off at a station stop called giving and never looked back.

Well, almost never. He did, after all, travel a fair distance in his own right on those tracks, spent nearly three decades, in fact, toiling in the financial canyons of Wall Street, moving from job to job up the executive ladder. He worked in the back offices and in the front offices of companies with names, reputations and changing fortunes large and small—Bache, E.F. Hutton, Shearson, Instanet. Toward the end of his career, he launched his own enterprise, a firm specializing in debt recovery for brokerage houses. "We did fine," he says, "until the market crashed and all of our contracts were pulled, and that was the end of that."

In 2000, at 62, he gave up the daily roller coaster, took a modest pension and retired—sort of. He and "Mrs. Claus" (Sharon, his wife of 22 years) embedded themselves more deeply than ever in community and church projects around their home base in Hamilton Square just beyond Trenton's city limits. For all practical purposes, though, not much has changed. Reilly still gets up every morning and goes to work, but he wouldn't have it any other way. "Why do I do this? Because it's fun," he says, using that word again. "I can make a little contribution to the world, and have a good time doing it. Besides, you meet a lot of interesting people."

At TASK, Reilly's involvement takes him far and wide. He commands the soup kitchen's delivery van, having stepped into the breach one day when the organization's regular full-time driver fell ill. After a while, the circuitous running of errands and the daily forays to collect food donated by area bakeries, grocery stores and the food bank became an open-ended assignment, and the soup kitchen, out of fairness, put him on the payroll. When not shuttling around in the van, he tutors students in TASK's adult education program. When not tutoring, he dishes out meals on the serving line. Or takes patrons to medical appointments. Or helps Sharon and other volunteers in the rear pantry. Or chaperones field trips. Or jokes with patrons and staff. Or answers the phone (indeed, his is the recorded voice you hear when you dial TASK's main number).

"I do whatever needs to be done," he says, likening the multi-task niche he has carved out to that of a baseball player adept at different positions on the field. "I'm the utility infielder."

•   •   •

A native New Yorker, Reilly grew up during the forties in the working class environs of Sheepshead Bay in Brooklyn and learned about need and compassion and interesting people at an early age. When he was 11, his father died after a long illness, and his mother, a homemaker, abruptly faced the uncertain prospect of having to find work to support Tom and his younger brother. "She got a job at Tetley Tea in the warehouse district on Canal Street in the city," he recalls, "and she went in at 11 o'clock at night and got home at 7 o'clock in the morning. She worked those hours because she wanted to be home during the day with us." He remembers what it was like to be in a family with someone working and still be poor, and "how my mother would help the neighbors and how they would help her." One Thanksgiving, in particular, sticks in his mind. "We had two turkeys given to us, one from the St. Vincent DePaul Society, another that just turned up in a basket on our front steps. My mother cooked up one of them, and we took it to this little elderly lady who had nothing and was living in a basement apartment. She got the extra turkey. One hand helps the other."

He also remembers being gripped by the realization that others were caught up in worse straits. "One time, I was in the back of a car—I don't even know how old I was; this was probably around 1948 or '49—and we came off the Manhattan Bridge and turned into the Bowery and it was twilight and there were all these dark lumps all over the place. In some of the doorways, there were piles. Along the divider down the middle of the street, people were laying along both sides of the fence. I mean they were just everywhere, hundreds, thousands maybe, and it went on for blocks. Someone said, 'Those are bums, derelicts, whatever.' I was just stunned."

After high school, Reilly worked his way in fits and starts through Brooklyn College, interrupting his studies at one point for a stint in the Air Force. Returning to school in the late 50s—and now married—he gravitated toward a major in education, figuring he had talent for the classroom. But then life intervened. His wife gave birth to a daughter, and "by the time I got enough credits for student teaching, I was already making $12,000 a year on Wall Street, while teaching was paying $3,000." It wasn't an altogether difficult choice.

•   •   •

Throughout his career in the financial district, Reilly made a habit of striking up conversations with street people, mainly on his way to work and during lunch. "I like people; I'm a talker," he says. "And in the course of various jobs, I'd walk around Trinity Church where the homeless and poor hung out, and I got friendly with a few of them. One lady was pretty interesting. She was in her 50s or 60s, hair all white, and she'd stand there with a Styrofoam cup, stand up against the wall of a building saying, 'Change! Change!' And I'd walk by and say things like 'How are you? How's it going?' And there would be no reaction, no comment whatsoever. Just 'Change!'

"About two years went by and one day she said, 'I'm fine.' Just like that. Eventually, we had a good chat, and one of the things she told me was this: 'On the welfare check I get I can either eat or pay rent. I can't do both. So I decided to eat, and then I panhandled enough for two six-packs, and with two six-packs you can sleep anywhere.'"

Encounters like that served him well when he got to the soup kitchen. At the suggestion of TASK's adult education coordinator, Kelly Hansen—who already knew Reilly through a mutual church affiliation—he joined the organization's corps of volunteer tutors. In that capacity, he spends at least three mornings a week hunkered down in one-on-one sessions that range from basic literacy instruction to courses in algebra and geometry for students on track for a Graduate Equivalency Diploma. "Many people we teach are in their 30s and 40s, and the fact that they come here at all means they're taking a risk. Think about it. You're 45 years old, and you're admitting you don't know your basic numbers or maybe even how to write," he says. "So they feel guilty about being here in the first place, and it probably took them a long time to work their way into coming, and they don't react well to stress.

"What they need most is to get past the sticking point, past the point where they start tightening up and saying the hell with this. If they make mistakes, you show them it's okay to make mistakes. I make more mistakes than they do, and they catch me in my mistakes, and they laugh. That's what I do. I'm very good at laughing them through it."

He appreciates what they have taught him as well, especially in the context of keeping an open mind. "During the first four or five months I was here, I tried to guess people's backgrounds, what they did, why they were here. I remember there was this one fellow and what stuck in my mind was that he looked quite comfortable, looked like he'd taken care of his own needs. Well, this was during a cold spell in January, and it was in the 20s every day and I asked him, 'Where are you sleeping?' and he said, 'I sleep under the bridge; I've been doing that for three years.' I asked him if he needed anything and he said, 'No, not me, but I'll check with the other guys.' Now I know there are a whole lot of people living under the bridges, living in the woods along the water in shacks they build there, in cars, whatever. I used to make judgments about people here, and I was wrong every time. I don't do that anymore."

Early in 2006, TASK submitted Tom's name for consideration in the Jefferson Award competition, an annual program designed to recognize exceptional volunteerism. Kelly Hansen prepared a letter of nomination to the award's local sponsor, *The Times* of Trenton. "I think that one of Tom's unique qualities is his desire and ability to get people to work together," she wrote. "He has encouraged some of our students at TASK to join him in delivering meals to homeless families through a local nonprofit, HomeFront. This allows our adult students the experience of giving rather than receiving help.

"Those who have participated have expressed surprise at how rewarding it was to give."

•

The Picture Lady

Exactly when the first piece came in, no one can say for sure, and anyway, it must have seemed a fluke at the time, totally unexpected, something right out of the blue. But then another one turned up. And another. And, well, they just keep coming. Works of art, all sorts, unsolicited and unbidden, and apparently unlimited, keep walking through TASK's front door: drawings, sketches, paintings, collages, portraits—gems of brush and color, pen and pencil, all riding currents of creativity and expression that will not be denied. Sometimes, they arrive on a whisper in the sheepish grip of the artists themselves. More often, delivery takes the form of an abrupt hand-off by a friend or relative on the way to grab a meal. Whatever the case, once inside, the person these couriers usually ask for is Susan Ellen—though not necessarily by that name. "Sometimes, there will be a note," she says, a smile crossing her face. "It'll say something like, 'Give this to the picture lady and tell her to hang it up.' Or sometimes, someone will come in and say, 'My brother or my sister is house-bound but does beautiful art. Can you come and see it?' And I'll go out and do that.

"I always ask, 'How did you hear about this?' And they say, 'On the street. Everybody knows there's art at the soup kitchen.'"

That's putting it mildly. There is so much art at TASK the building presents itself as a sort of free-form gallery with a cafeteria on the side, virtually every inch of available wall space in the dining area covered by the framed and matted works of self-styled local Picassos and Rembrandts, a veritable extravaganza of color and fancy and imagination in a most unlikely place. So much art that a good deal of it has to be held in storage. Indeed, so much, says the picture lady, that combined with the frames, paper, canvass, paint and myriad other supplies offered by generous donors, some of which she stores at home, "my own house has been turned into a warehouse. I don't know what I'm going to do. We'll just have to find more places around Trenton that will let us hang our art because it's being produced every week."

Aside from the walk-in talent—which in some ways, she says, is the most gratifying part because it evidences a clear connection to the wider surrounding community—the bulk of the artwork is churned out by a regular circle of contributors who pursue aesthetic aspirations at their own pace through loosely structured arts and photography programs offered at TASK under her volunteer guidance. The crown jewel of the whole painterly enterprise is a self-sustaining group of self-taught artists who, for all intents and purposes, have gone professional. They call themselves the A-Team Artists of Trenton, and their work frequently is on display in other venues. More to the point, it often sells in an arts-and-crafts marketplace that prizes so-called "outsider art," what the French artist Jean Dubuffet characterized four decades ago as *Art Brut*, or raw art—works unadorned and unadulterated by structured technique or mainstream influence. "Some of these people," Susan says, "are as serious artists as you will find anywhere, and they are very good."

And to think it all began with a paper hat, a few feathers and handful of bells.

•   •   •

In 1988, when she first showed up at TASK, Susan was in the prime of a career about as far removed from painting and poverty as you could get. A child of some privilege who grew up in New York City and New Rochelle, she never had any formal training in fine arts, though, as a child, "I always loved art, and whenever there were exhibits I was in them." She gravitated instead toward the sciences, specifically to psychology, earning degrees from Mount Holyoke and Barnard and a doctorate in experimental social psychology from New York University.

She went on to teach and conduct research at Princeton University while offering clinical therapy on the side, and, by the late 80s, had married, started a family and was deeply engaged in a busy, comfortable, professionally fulfilling life.

After a while, maybe a little too comfortable.

"I guess I was settled enough, and I was really feeling a little constrained by, or at least familiar enough with, the classroom setting and with the clinical setting," she says. "I just came down [to TASK] because I was curious. I wanted to know how people in poverty manage, what life is like and how you survive on the street. It was always something I was interested in, and it was just in the back of my mind. I also wanted to learn something about myself: if I put myself into a setting where there were people under stress, under-served, could I turn on a dime? Not to do therapy—that is definitely not what I'm doing here. But did I have the skills that people could draw on? Could I interact in maybe a therapeutic way?

"My goal was not to come down with an agenda. It was to just put myself into the situation and go in whatever direction people asked me to go."

At the time, TASK was operating out of space leased from the Salvation Army on East State Street while awaiting completion of a permanent home across town, and the day Susan walked in they put her to work at the tail end of the food-service line. "I was the cream and sugar person," she recalls. "It was a great position since my interest was in interacting with people, and after a doing that for a while, I'd remember names—you know, who would take two sugars and one cream, that sort of thing. Then, I'd be out somewhere, at the train station or some place, and run into someone who would say, 'Hey, you know what I take!' and I'd say, 'Yeah, light and sweet!'"

There was one thing, though, that Susan simply could not bring herself to abide: wearing one of those plain, soda jerk-style paper hygiene hats. "I look ugly in hats anyway, but I had to wear this one and so I decided to decorate it. I used feathers, bells, that sort of thing." (Recounting this, she adds as an aside, "You can tell I'm an old hippie!") Before long, Patricia Dorsey, then TASK's director, "came to me and asked, 'Ah, about the hat—you seem to have something of a creative streak, how about making some signs for the soup kitchen describing our services?'

"That was a really interesting challenge. I knew there were literacy problems and so the question was could I make visually stimulating posters that would convey the sense and meaning of the services without necessarily using words?" As Susan set about trying to tackle it, working before and after meals, a curious thing started to happen. "Kids would come in, and they wanted to help. I said, 'Sure, I can use all the help I can get.' And then the adults started coming around. And we'd all sit around doing artwork." In short order, the posters got done, but it didn't stop there. Soup kitchen staffers saw an opportunity to use arts-related activities as a kind of magnet for child nutrition. Gather some colored markers, crayons, paper and other rudimentary supplies together with toys and books in a small room behind the director's office, Susan says, and "maybe it would encourage parents to bring their children in for meals. So I started doing that; every Tuesday, they took me off the line to run this."

One such Tuesday, a woman approached holding an infant. "The baby was lame, and she really doted on this child, and she asked if I would take her picture. So I went out to my car in the glove compartment and got my kids' little point-and-shoot, which is what I still use today, and I took a picture of her baby." Susan developed the photos herself, presented them to the woman, and word soon spread: there is this person down at the soup kitchen who will snap a photo-portrait of you for free, no questions asked. "It's really interesting what pictures do for people," she says. "For some, it's the first time they've ever seen an image of themselves captured on film, and they'll say, 'Oh, look at me!'"

And with that, the "picture lady"—"my street name!" says Susan—was born.

•   •   •

A year or so later, after TASK had settled into its new and larger digs on Escher Street, the *ad hoc* arts effort was organized into a more expansive program dubbed "Extra Helpings" that boasted three core elements for all age groups—"Kids' Time," the original component built around art, play and reading; "Arts and Ideas," which combined artwork, poetry and literature with free-wheeling conversation and discussion; and "Photo Ops," in which participants could experiment with cameras.

For Susan, every day was an eye-opener, particularly when it came to the children. She had little difficulty securing basic supplies—"You can go around at 4 o'clock in the afternoon to garage sales on the weekend and people want to get rid of things, and I get them for a dime or for nothing." But books were another matter entirely. "I started looking around for books that kids in second and third grade could take home, and it was very difficult to find any for these children," she says. "You know, there would be books about white kids' birthday parties, adventures with a pet, animals in the woods, that sort of thing, but not much that related to these children's lives." As it turned out, that was the least of the obstacles. When she did manage to assemble a small library, the stark face of illiteracy reared up again. "Some of the parents couldn't read them, and they would get so frustrated." Susan also wondered why, when it came to the various toys she collected, kids who came to TASK would gravitate toward things like the *faux* doctor's bag and kit. As she got to know the children better, she discovered such items were popular due mainly to their familiarity. "These kids were spending so much time in emergency rooms. I started finding out that something as simple as diarrhea can keep a parent with a kid in a hospital emergency room for a day. These were all things that were new to me. This is what I wanted to learn." More recently, her instruction along these lines has taken a somewhat more disturbing turn. It used to be that limited space in TASK's modest multi-purpose room was a chronic problem because of the number of children who would turn out for any given session of Kids' Time. Not anymore. "There's been a real drop-off," she says. "I started asking around and found that there's one good reason for that and one not so good. There are more day-care options and summer programs now, and that's good. The sad reason is that gangs have become so prevalent that people don't want to walk here with their kids because it's dangerous."

In spite of that trend, the soup kitchen had already established itself as a haven for creativity, its very walls offering an advertisement of that fact and a standing invitation to children and adults alike. That was Susan's idea, too. "As soon as I got a chance, I started hanging the artwork," she says. "I just thought, this is a community place, why not? They took so much pride in their photographs and in their drawings and paintings, let's make this place theirs—put it on display so they can look around and see all the talent they've expressed." Soon, others started taking notice as well, including volunteers who showed up thinking they would just be serving food to the needy but instead found themselves drawn to the surrounding display. "People came in," she says, "and started asking if any of it was for sale." Then came offers, particularly from area churches—notably Nassau Presbyterian in Princeton—to display soup kitchen works in venues outside Trenton. For one such early exhibition, Alicia Nieves, the owner of a small gallery in Rocky Hill just north of Princeton placed her space at TASK's disposal, and the result was a very successful little show. That event holds a special place in the memories of participants not just because it was a first but also because of a tragic yet poignant series of circumstances that followed. After the opening, the soup kitchen artists were shocked to learn that Nieves was killed in an automobile accident. Her funeral, an informal gathering held in the home of a relative, "was one of those affairs where anybody could stand up and say something, and the artists wanted so much to go," Susan recalls. "So we drove up, and we were in the back, very unobtrusive. And one of the artists stood up to talk, and it was so touching. She talked about what it meant to her to be there and that she was from the soup kitchen. And then another stood up. And afterwards, people just flocked to them and were so grateful that they had come."

•   •   •

Sometime in 2001, it became readily apparent that not only was Extra Helpings beginning to outgrow the soup kitchen with its surfeit of artwork and burgeoning storage needs, but also that some of the artists were on the verge of outgrowing the program. What had begun as a sort of hobby had matured into a serious vocation, and a core group of a half-dozen or so regulars started exploring ways to employ their skills as the basis for launching an independent business partnership. Much discussion ensued, and what finally emerged was a cooperative organized under a name borrowed from a once-popular television series about a band of lovable army rogues who came to the aid of people in distress. Not everyone got it at first. "I said, 'What does that have to do with art?'" Susan recalls. "They said, 'Well, the A Team did good things, and we do good things, and 'A' could stand for Art.' They just liked the strength of it." Thus, the A-Team Artists of Trenton was up and running.

But a name was one thing. The next step was a bit more challenging—Could the new enterprise grow its own financial legs? TASK's governing board bet yes and backed its words with a $4,000 loan. Within less than two years, flush from the sale of posters, greeting cards and other creative and appealing examples of entrepreneurial artwork, the verdict was in: the A-Team artists presented the board with a check, the first installment toward paying off the note and a major leap toward their ultimate goal of self-sufficiency. "The soup kitchen is our home base and generously donates space," says Susan, "but the budget is our own."

If there is one aspect of the venture that seems to appeal to the group more than anything else, sometimes even more than making a sale, she says, it is the regular and ever-widening platform of public exposure afforded by being part of an established entity. Beyond the walls of the soup kitchen, works produced by the team are or have been put on display in galleries, schools, nursing homes, senior centers and corporate venues, including the sprawling Lawrenceville office campus of the Bristol Myers-Squibb Corp. Exhibitions have been held in art centers as far north as Woodbridge, and a poster nationally commemorating the

40th anniversary of the launch of the Medicaid health-insurance program—featuring poetry and graphic art by Annabelle Rose, a celebrated founding A-Team artist who died in 2005 after a long struggle with homelessness and cancer—was chosen to grace select clinics across America. "You'd think money would be a big deal," says Susan, "but it's not. It's 'somebody likes my art.' I mean, my jaw would drop—we'd be somewhere and somebody would say, 'How much is that?', and the artist would set a price, say $35. And the person would say, 'Uh, I don't have that much.' And the artist would say, 'Just take it then.' At one of the early art shows one of the artists came up to me and said, 'See that lady over there? She bought one of my pictures and said some day, she'll be old and sick and she'll look up on the wall and see my picture and feel happy.' That's what this is about."

Herman Rose, known to all as Shorty, is a 53-year-old man who was drawn into the arts programs and onto to the A-Team by his sister, the late Annabelle. His specialty is hand-crafted picture frames, which he fashions by folding colorful paper, plastic and cloth into small squares and weaving them together. They sell for $25 and up. "But sometimes I just like to do it and get my work out there," he says. "Let people see how my work is." He keeps a scrapbook full of photographs of each piece he produces and takes it with him on various A-Team field trips to museums and to the studios of artists who invite the group for tours and seminars. "That makes my heart jump—to see other people's work," Shorty says.

On the wall behind him in TASK's art room is a selection of drawings and paintings, including a textured oil landscape by Jean Davis, an A-Teamer who until a year or so ago "had never painted in my life. And Susan was like, 'Just do anything.' And I just started turning in artwork, and it took off from there. "I really like the natural feel of my pictures." Davis, 60, a former home health aide, suffers from lupus and has been on disability for several years. "I've had to live with this disease for ten years. It's a lot to deal with, very painful. So it's hard, and painting just kind of takes away the stress, fills the gap. It's opened up a doorway for me."

The A-Team's ranks have grown even to include volunteers. Lorna Lorraine started lending a hand at TASK in 2003, "and when I saw the artwork on the walls and what they were doing, it blew me away and inspired me to try it myself." She works in pastels, producing portraits rich with deep, vibrant colors. "I never envisioned myself as artist," says Lorraine, who also dabbles in poetry during her time off from work as an aide at Trenton Psychiatric Hospital. "It's a high-stress environment, and I needed an outlet. This keeps me going. We all support each other on the A-Team. Everybody brings something different to the table. You can look at people's work and tell who did it because everybody has their own unique style. It's really amazing. I think we're the best kept secret in Trenton."

.   .   .

If you ask Susan about her approach to volunteering and what she has learned after all these years at TASK, you should expect to hear something of the unexpected in her response. That's because, in large measure, the unexpected is precisely what she herself found in this place.

"I'm not here because I feel like I'm doing something good for other people," she says matter-of-factly. "I'm not good enough myself to do that. And I'm very suspicious of that motive. If you need to help people, maybe you need them to need help. I want them *not* to need help. That's not to denigrate others' motives—you know, guided by a higher power, doing it because their value system or their religion promotes it. That's fine; I think it's great. And I'm glad if what I do does help. It certainly helps me. But I don't have any sense of sacrifice about this. I'm just here because it's interesting, and I like it." She is also extremely uncomfortable with the notion of personal notoriety, of drawing attention to herself, which is why she had to be coaxed into sitting for an interview and then asked that her real last name not be used here. It's not just shyness. "When I'm at the soup kitchen, that's not who I am," she says. "I like being known as 'the picture lady.' It's an important part of my experience there."

She is not a religious person, either, at least not in the conventional sense. Indeed, she describes herself as "very unspiritual," raised in the Jewish tradition but long ago lapsed. Working at TASK, though, prompted a reassessment, if not a reawakening, and it surprised her. "This is the first place in my whole life where I've really seen religion have a powerful force in people's lives," Susan says. She was drawn to that recognition, in part, by the simple, unaffected devotion shown by people she has met in their struggle to cope with life and death. "Every month, people we know at the soup kitchen die, and I will get requests from the family to attend the funeral service. It's usually an open casket, and they want a picture of how beautiful the person looks. In one case, I made a whole photo book. It was a child who I knew from before she was born until when she died of cancer at nine years old.

"You see it on a human level here," she says. "Take drug addiction. Of course, I always knew about it as a psychologist, but here it becomes understandable. You see how hard people fight to get out of the rut and the many things that are stacked against them. They'll come in and they'll be clean for a while, and they feel so good, and God has helped—religion, they're hanging onto it like a lifeline. And it's so genuine."

Susan also found herself quite "stunned when I first came down here—and still am—at the generosity of spirit. I expected some hostility, some resentment, and it's not here. In some ways, I'm much more comfortable down here than in Princeton. It's in your face, it's quick, it's unpredictable, it's honest—you know, what you see is what you get. If somebody's pissed off at you, you know it. If somebody loves you, you know it. Right away."

But what she was most unprepared for, what has left her most pleasantly surprised, is a growing sense that TASK has helped her complete a circle.

"As I look back on my life, it makes so much sense that I wound up here. I mean, as a child, I wanted to be an artist, and then I became a psychologist, which I also love, and it's funny how it's come together. This is a perfect combination, and it happened with no plan whatsoever.

And so far, it seems to be weaving together the basic strands of my life in a way that I would never have expected."

•

Emilio

Early one September evening a few years ago, Emilio Papa was finishing a few chores at the soup kitchen when a woman approached asking for help. He recognized her because she had spoken to him on other occasions about different matters, mainly about losing her job and trying to get back on track. She had some experience in nursing, she told him, and wondered whether someone could point her in the right direction. Emilio was no stranger to this sort of thing. A longtime volunteer, he had taken a special interest in people who showed up not only hungry for food but also for work. He would give them a hand with job applications, even drive them to interviews. So he chatted with this woman for several minutes and told her that, based upon their earlier conversations, he had collected a batch of material about health-care job opportunities and training in the Trenton area. Meanwhile, with the evening meal winding down and the soup kitchen about to close for the day, she asked if he would take her to get something to eat. Emilio had done that sort of thing before, too, and he readily offered his company.

And with that, he demonstrated—albeit unwittingly and perhaps, as subsequent events would suggest, a trifle foolishly—just how far some TASK volunteers are willing to go to lend a hand.

They left the soup kitchen, got into his car and drove out of the city, heading north on Route 1 toward a Red Lobster in Lawrenceville. At some point during the meal, Emilio exited the restaurant to retrieve the paperwork for her. "I opened the car door," he says, "and then I felt something hit the top of my head, and that's all I remember." He woke the next day in a hospital bed with a badly bruised and bandaged face, a swollen jaw and the type of headache that only a concussion can produce. The exact circumstances surrounding the mugging were murky.

The woman, located by police later that evening and found to be in possession of Emilio's wallet, was taken into custody on the suspicion that, at the very least, she had been an accomplice to some unknown assailant. But there were no witnesses, and Emilio, unable to say for sure if any money was missing, declined to press charges.

When news of the assault reached TASK, it was greeted with a mixture of concern and consternation. Here was one sweet guy, they said, but what in the world was he doing driving around alone at night with someone who, for all practical purposes, was a perfect stranger? At five-foot nine and thin as a rail—*and verging on 80 years of age, not to mention having survived cancer and heart surgery, for crying out loud!*—he's lucky he wasn't injured more seriously, or worse.

But were they shocked? Not really. No one who knows this energetic, gentle man with the quavering voice and the owlish expression could possibly have been entirely surprised. After all, he is a veritable TASK fixture, has been for going on 25 years, practically symbolizes the spirit of the place by his almost daily presence. At one time or another, he has had a hand in everything from serving food to serving on the organization's board of trustees. Aside from all of that, it doesn't take any great power of observation to notice that his favorite part is mingling with the staff and with those who give him a reason for being there in the first place, and he has no compunction about doing what he thinks is necessary to give them a boost. Which is why, after he recovered, and it was politely suggested that he consider curtailing his freelance employment-counseling activities in favor of the official channels, it wasn't easy for him.

"I was trying to help," he says, squinting through those big, round black-framed glasses he wears. "You know, I just thought that if I could find work for them, at least they'd be on their own."

·   ·   ·

Charity and self-reliance.

Emilio discovered the inextricable connection between the two early in life on the streets of Chambersburg, a predominantly Italian working-class enclave in south Trenton where helping neighbors was second nature. This was in the 20s and early 30s when homes in the city were still heated with wood or coal, modern appliances were few and far between, and a family's daily bread depended, literally, on access to a local baker's ovens. Born in the middle of six brothers and four sisters, he remembers his mother preparing dough early in the morning in their Mott Street row house and sending him and a few siblings off to a bakery that charged a few pennies to bake the entire batch. "And not just for us," he says. "She would make extra for the poor. Two or three hours later, we would go back and pick up the bread and take some of it to five or six different homes of people she knew who needed it." But there was "poor," and there was poor, and sometimes, the need was closer to home. Emilio's father held a steady job at the Trenton Pottery Company, a leading manufacturer of porcelain bathroom fixtures, but his family occasionally had to turn to the generosity of others as well. "We used to go up to the Armory where they gave out flour and sugar. At Christmas, we could each get one toy there. It was a kind of relief program for us."

When he speaks of those days, Emilio sometimes takes a nickel from the coin purse of his worn leather wallet and tells this story: "When I was a little boy, about seven years old, my grandmother passed away, and I volunteered to stay with my grandfather, take care of him, you know, chop wood, make sure he got enough to eat. One day, he gave me five cents and sent me to church. He said, 'I want you to put this in the offering basket.' I said, 'But Grandpa, I worked all week for this five cents, and you're telling me to give it away?' He said, 'Do what I tell you,' and so I went and I held onto it until the basket came around and I finally put it in. And that's the five cents I figured that started my life because the next week I had 10 cents in my pocket. I learned that when you give of yourself, you're going to receive more than what you gave."

Somewhere along the line, Emilio also learned a life-lesson about prejudice—in a way that has resonated through the years. Trembling at the thought, he recalls encountering a certain streak of mean-spiritedness toward those who rely on places like soup kitchens. He got

involved with TASK after seeing people climbing into dumpsters looking for food just blocks from New Jersey's Statehouse. It seemed to him
like the most natural thing in the world to do in response to the obvious
need. But then he heard words he never thought he'd hear. "I don't want
to say it because it makes me so agitated, but people have said things
like, 'Emilio, are you still serving those ...?' I don't even want to say
the word they use. It puts tears in my eyes. I can't believe people say
things like that. But when you do something from your heart, you don't
listen to other people's remarks."

As to formal education, his ended with eighth grade. "I had to work
for my family," he says. He took odd jobs, whatever he could find, to
bring in a few extra dollars each week—shining shoes, hawking newspapers, selling groceries, hauling meat in a butcher shop. In the process,
he became skilled with the tools of several trades. What he really
wanted, though, was to become a cop—but not just any cop. Emilio
wanted to be a "G-man," an agent of the Federal Bureau of Investigation, his interest whetted by a State Police captain who came into the
store where he was working one day and wound up becoming a sort of
mentor. Emilio toured State Police headquarters and enrolled in finger-
print technology courses offered by a Chicago-based correspondence
school called the Institute of Applied Science. Visions of a trip to Washington and a career in specialized law enforcement danced in his head.

Then it all went south amid a cascade of intervening circumstances.

In 1943, having reached draft age in the middle of a raging global
war, Emilio enlisted in the Army. Within six months, after a troubled
stint in boot camp where he developed debilitating problems with his
feet, he was forced to take a medical discharge. "I didn't make out too
good there," he says, "but I figured I could still do something to serve
my country." Upon returning home, he dug out a letter he had received
from none other than J. Edgar Hoover himself (whose legend was built,
in part, on a penchant for personal replies) in response to an inquiry
about the FBI's recruitment needs. But as he started prepping for the
application process, it soon became apparent that he was running a losing race against a dream. His brothers had also gone into the service,

and no one was left to support the family. Emilio was elected, and, in what played out as a kind of true-life version of the experience endured by the fictional George Bailey in *It's A Wonderful Life*, Emilio stayed behind to fight the battle of Trenton.

Not that his interest in sleuthing and law enforcement went totally unrequited. In the post-war years, he landed a job as a security officer with Chase Aircraft, a West Trenton-based maker of military transports. His duties included taking fingerprints from prospective employees and running them up to the State Police for analysis as part of background checks. After a few years, he took a higher-paying security job at the Naval Air Propulsion Center in Ewing, and that is where he spent the next 34 years—with one exception. In the early 50s, he was recalled temporarily to Chase's employ to help with an investigation of mysterious circumstances surrounding damage to aircraft parts. "They were finding aluminum shavings in some of the engines, and they borrowed me back from the Navy to help out," he says. The probe eventually led to the dismissal and arrest of an employee on charges of sabotage.

•   •   •

These days, Emilio lives by himself in a rambling ranch-style brick house off Route 31 in Pennington, a Trenton suburb just north of the city. He built the place with his own hands in 1955 and moved in the following year with his bride, Rose. She died in 2005, just before their 50th wedding anniversary. They never had children, and though he still has family in the area—a sister and a couple of his brothers live nearby—sometimes he is lonely. "Sometimes," he says, "I get up at four in the morning, and I pray. That's where I come from." He likes listening to opera, too. "And I stay busy. People say, 'Emilio, when are you going to retire?' I tell them, 'First, I'm not a senior citizen, and second, I don't have time to retire.'"

Much of that time is spent back in the city. If he's not looking for something to do at the soup kitchen, he's involved in local American Legion activities or helping give Sunday communion to patients at St. Francis Hospital or serving meals two Saturdays every month through a church-sponsored feed-the-hungry program called Loaves and Fishes at St. Mary's Cathedral. One of his favorite pastimes is tinkering with a collection of carnival-style games, more than two dozen in all—pinball bowling, mini-golf, a ring toss, a wheel of fortune, even a six-foot-tall dunk tank featuring a gangly stuffed animal as the victim—that he has assembled from scraps of wood and other material over the years for use at charity fundraisers. "It's like a hobby," he says. "I get these different ideas, and whatever comes into my head I start to work on it."

For the time being, Emilio, a devout Catholic, wants to convert his backyard into "a prayer garden for my wife, to honor her." He calls it "my next assignment." Coming from a guy who has survived heart surgery and cancer, not to mention the odd mugging, who is going to bet he won't complete it?

Epilogue

Once a year, TASK turns the tables on its volunteers, throwing open the house and inviting them to sit down for a change and enjoy a buffet luncheon in recognition of all they do. The 2007 edition of this "big thank you," marking a quarter-century of service by the organization and its loyal corps of magnanimous helpers, took place on a sparkling Saturday afternoon in mid-April, the sun so bright, the cloudless sky so blue and the air so soft and warm on the heels of a late-lingering winter that even the mean streets of the city's far north end seemed to reflect a promising glint of renewal.

Greeted at the door with smiles, guests were handed name tags and keepsake navy-blue aprons embossed with the soup kitchen's logo. Small posters dangling from strings fixed to the ceiling panels displayed an honor roll of schools, churches, clubs, businesses and other sources of generous hands-on assistance provided during the previous 12 months. The dining area, meanwhile, was transformed. Dressed in paper covers and sprouting colorful centerpiece arrangements donated by local florists, the tables bore eight settings of salad bowls, plastic flatware and napkins, one place mat discreetly tagged with a green dot to signify who among the as-yet unsuspecting diners at each table would be lucky enough to take the flowers home.

As the kitchen staff scurried through final preparations and a group of students from suburban Hamilton High School, today's servers, moved among the small murmuring crowd offering coffee, tea, juice and water, the event took on the quiet rhythm of past volunteer luncheons, an easy mix of warmth and fellowship with a dash of continuity. And that was a good thing, because despite the overwhelming familiarity of the circumstance and the surroundings—the smell of the kitchen, the embracing walls of artwork, the shared sense of community and service—there were obvious signs that TASK was not altogether the same place it had been even weeks earlier. Change was riding in on the spring breeze, silently yet with a force that could not be denied, tugging at the people gathered there, transforming the building they were in, rearranging and altering both the tools and the administrators of their charitable trade—starting right at the top.

For the better part of a decade, the man at the microphone voicing words of welcome at affairs like this had been Peter Wise, whose stewardship as executive director saw TASK grow from a mom-and-pop-sized relief operation into a well-oiled, integral component of the Trenton region's social-service spectrum. It was a good run—eight years-plus at the helm, an unparalleled tenure of leadership for the organization. But late in 2006, Peter decided it was time for a breather, time to move on and, so, in March, he retired. He returned today, accompanied by his wife Kathy, and clearly enjoyed the moment and the memories, taking it all in from a new perspective: a seat among the volunteers he had come to know so well.

When the time came for introductions, Dennis Micai, the soup kitchen's new leader, stepped to the podium and laid on a hefty helping of self-deprecating humor. A huge football fan, he likened the circumstance of his arrival to that of the fellow some years ago who succeeded legendary Green Bay Packers football coach Vince Lombardi. "Nobody remembers who that guy was," Micai said, dead-panning "That's kind of how I felt coming in." The line was an apt ice-breaker, drawing laughs and scattered applause, but anyone familiar with the new director's resume knows it's impossible to sell him short. With nearly 40 years of public service under his belt, Micai's credentials include extensive experience running local organizations who share the mission of helping the less fortunate, including the Mercer County Board of Social Services and the ARC/Mercer, a nonprofit entity devoted to serving the disabled. In addition to many other endeavors, he has also volunteered in various capacities at TASK over the years and knows the organization well; indeed, he was recruited to fill the soup kitchen's top job while serving as a member its governing board. He spends a good deal of time listening rather than talking, and he's particularly interested in hearing sensible suggestions about ways to collaborate with other groups in order to reach under-served areas of the city. That said, Micai's ultimate goal, at least from the standpoint of attacking hunger, is about as ambitious and idealistic as you can get in this line of work: to eliminate the need for soup kitchens in the first place. "I guess I'm pleased, and not so pleased, that we'll be adding a forth nightly meal at South Trenton in May," he told the assembled volunteers, announcing expanded food service at a satellite facility across town operated by TASK in conjunction with local churches. "While it's a good thing we'll be able to do another meal there, it's also a sad commentary on the times."

Meanwhile, as to the immediate challenge of transitioning into the soup kitchen's saddle, it's been so far, so good, though a few minor glitches have tangled him up along the way. Micai regaled his table mates with but one example, a sort of rite of initiation into the unpredictable, often quirky nature of running this place. It happened late one afternoon barely three weeks into the job. Typically the last person to leave at the end of the day, Micai neglected on this particular occasion to make a final check of the restrooms before locking up and arming the electronic burglar detection system. About to drive off in his car, he heard that very alarm blaring away and looked up to observe a peculiar sight: a man on the sidewalk wildly waving his arms—the off-duty police officer who had provided security at the soup kitchen that very day. The guy had been in the men's room changing clothes when Micai exited and unwittingly triggered the alarm on his way out. Minutes later, some of the moonlighting cop's on-duty colleagues arrived to investigate, their presence quickly followed by a tedious rash of phone calls to straighten things out with the alarm company. "My welcome to the soup kitchen!" TASK's new chief said with a burst of chagrined laughter.

With that, Micai handed the microphone over to another new face whose owner lately has brought fresh style and energy to one of TASK's most demanding and critical roles. She is Ann Orth, and in the space of several months, she has gone from apron-wearing volunteer to full-time employee *in charge* of volunteers. A pharmaceutical executive with an eclectic academic background in music and biology, Ann decided in late 2006 after devoting considerable time to TASK that, spiritually, it was time to put her skills to work along a different career path. With active encouragement from Wise and others, she applied for the job of volunteer and patron services director, and now spends her days in command of the recruitment, deployment and care and feeding of the organization's most precious commodity—the very people arrayed before her at this moment. It's been a good fit all around. "The job is rewarding on many different levels," she said, "and I know I can, and have, made a difference in many lives." And even though she's still navigating her own learning curve—matching so many names and faces on a regular basis is daunting in itself, let alone assuring the presence of adequate volunteers on a daily basis—she wouldn't have it any other way. "There are 19 of us on/staff and almost 800 of you and we really count of your support," Ann told the volunteers. "And, I promise, I'll learn all your names eventually!"

Soon, she and other staffers will have to get busy laying plans for a more extensive orientation tour of the soup kitchen as well. Behind and to the right of her, mounted on a small easel in full view of everyone—in plain sight, so to speak—stood a detailed architectural rendering of the TASK of the future, the blueprint for a major physical-plant expansion finally taking shape after years of planning and fund-raising—Hunger, Inc. on the march again.

A few weeks ago, the foundation was poured and the rebar set in place, and now walls of tan block were rising. The enlarged kitchen will be furnished with better and more efficient equipment, new walk-in freezer and cooler units will hold greater supplies of fresh food, expansive dry-storage areas will finally relieve the sorely overcrowded pantries and volunteers will have more room to sort, package, stock and distribute all manner of necessary items. Out front, more space will be set aside for TASK's arts and computer programs, the adult education crew will actually be able to move about without tripping over one another and their supplies, and a big new multi-purpose room will be available for counseling sessions, community meetings and other functions. The dining area proper is targeted for only a modest increase in size, and there's a good reason for that: the soup kitchen already turns out upwards of 600 meals a day, and given the complicated practical challenge of sustaining that level of service with limited staff and resources, the maximum number of people who can be comfortably and safely accommodated at any given time is finite.

As Micai took his audience on a virtual tour of the project highlights, he explained that the coming months promised to be hectic. Schedules might need adjustment, meal menus might have to be reconfigured temporarily during work on the kitchen, and it's likely that everyone will have to maneuver around periodic disruptions to parking, to building access and to some of the of activities offered by the organization on a daily basis—all part of the price of moving TASK to the next level.

But in the midst of all this change and transformation, there remains one abiding constant, and the volunteers were reminded of it by way of a simple story whose telling stood out among all the other words uttered this day.

One morning not long ago, it seems a young man came to TASK's adult education class feeling ill and out of sorts with a fever that suggested flu. As he sat at a table, his head cradled in his arms, his condition obviously worsening by the minute, someone decided to call for an ambulance. When it arrived, and he was placed on a stretcher, the emergency medical technicians were asked if someone from the soup kitchen could ride along with him to the hospital. Sorry, one of them said, family members only, or words to that effect. To which Cathy Ann Vandegrift, the organization's steadfast assistant director, replied, "But we *are* family." Just like that. No hesitation, no qualification. As natural and direct and true as the sun streaming through the windows.

Acknowledgments

T he completion of this book would not have been possible without help from many people, starting with the staff, patrons and volunteers of TASK. Special thanks to Dennis Micai, Peter Wise, Cathy Ann Vandegrift, Ann Orth, Sam Johnson, Kelly Hansen, Tom Reilly, Diane Subber, Jan Curran, Mary Ann Dobson, Anne Hamilton, Jaime Parker, Mike Mendez, Jennifer Brown and the entire kitchen and program staff for their enthusiasm and willingness to share thoughts and insights into the operations and work of an unparalleled organization. As to the storied history of this institution, it would have been impossible to set forth without invaluable input from Art and Barbara Stanley, Alice Parker, John and Terese Nelson, Beverly Mills, John Weatherly, Cynthia Krommes, John Valentine, Steve Leder and Marty Johnson.

Special appreciation goes to Marty Tuchman for his generous recognition of this as a worthy endeavor and to Irwin Stoolmacher for serving throughout as a sounding board and fact-checker and for lending his promotional skills. Both of these gentlemen are emblematic of the scores of compassionate and talented individuals who have assisted this organization and those it serves in countless ways over the years, including those with whom the author became personally acquainted, among them present and former members of TASK's Board of Trustees, including Ben Abeles, Linda Bell, Lesley Borges Carter, Stephen Chukumba, Susan E. Darley, Tracey Destribats, David Geltzer, Dave Gibbons, Michael Gluck, Peter Haas, Pamela Sims Jones, John Kelly, Doreeen Kornrumpf, Virginia Link, Sasa Montano, John Monteleone, Gloria Nevius, Marty Oppenheimer, Emilio Papa, Jim Parker, Joe Robinson, Sue Rodgers, Seenu Srinivasan, Henry Weiss, Kathy Wooley, Bob Workman, Jennifer Zeigler and Michelle Young.

Though the organization and its governing board played no role in the decision to undertake this book or in the shaping, writing or publishing of its contents, these individuals, along with many, many others who came before them, remain an inspiration, particularly to those who, hopefully, will follow in their footsteps.

Sources and Methods

G iven the grounding of this book in current events that involve real people, efforts were made whenever possible to gather material and insight directly from those who know the story of TASK and the hunger industry better than anyone—the workers, the volunteers and those they serve. Thus, more than three dozen in-depth personal interviews were conducted over a period of months and served as a primary source of information, with many such encounters requiring extensive follow-up work to verify facts and pursue new leads. In some instances, individuals are not fully identified either at their request or at the discretion of the author. In every case, extreme care was taken to present an accurate and faithful record. Thanks to all who gave so generously, thoughtfully and patiently of their time.

The author also reviewed hundreds of articles, editorials and analyses published over the years in various news media outlets, starting with Trenton's two longstanding newspapers, *The Times* and *The Trentonian*, as well as *The New York Times*, *The Wall Street Journal*, *The Washington Post*, *The Star-Ledger* of Newark, *The Record* of Hackensack, *The Chronicle of Philanthropy* and The Associated Press. Particularly helpful were the contents of a box of archival material collected by TASK over the years, including original letters and other documents and an extensive chronological file of newspaper clippings and other resource materials dating back to the organization's birth in the early 1980s.

In addition to TASK, the author consulted a wide range of other organizations both in the research and nonprofit communities and in government, including America's Second Harvest, the Association for Children of New Jersey, the Brookings Institution, the Center for American Progress, the Community FoodBank of New Jersey, the Economic Policy Institute, the Global Policy Forum, HomeFront, the Housing and Community Development Network of New Jersey, Isles Inc., Mercer Street Friends, New Jersey Policy Perspective, the Rescue Mission of Trenton, the New Jersey Department of Agriculture, the New Jersey Departments of Health and Human Services, the U.S. Bureau of Labor Statistics, the U.S. Census Bureau and the U.S. Department of Agriculture.

Except where otherwise noted or attributed, the statements and opinions expressed in the resulting narrative are the author's alone and do not necessarily reflect those of TASK or any other individual or organization.

978-0-595-42758-1
0-595-42758-8

Made in the USA